BIRCH

Reaktion's Botanical series is the first of its kind, integrating horticultural and botanical writing with a broader account of the cultural and social impact of trees, plants and flowers.

BIRCH

Anna Lewington

REAKTION BOOKS

For John, Eppie and Aaron

Published by
REAKTION BOOKS LTD
Unit 32, Waterside
44–48 Wharf Road
London N1 7UX, UK

www.reaktionbooks.co.uk

First published 2018

Printed and bound in China by 1010 Printing International Ltd

A catalogue record for this book is available from the British Library

ISBN 978 1 78914 011 8

Contents

A silver birch (*B. pendula*) in spring, Dorset, England.

Introduction

Elegant and beautiful, rich in history and supremely useful, birches have played an extraordinary yet largely unacknowledged part in shaping both our natural environment and the material culture and beliefs of millions of people around the world. Common throughout the cool parts of the northern hemisphere, birches are surely among the world's most easily recognized of trees. Their graceful shape and form, the delicacy of their foliage and their striking, tactile bark have helped some species to become as well loved as they are widely known – from the silver birches (*Betula pendula*) of Europe, characterized by their famously weeping habit, to intensely white-barked Himalayan trees or the paper birch (*B. papyrifera*) which ranges across North America from the Atlantic to the Pacific coast.

For hundreds of thousands of years, adept at dodging ice sheets and aided by their tiny wind-borne seeds, birches have been environmental pioneers, rapidly colonizing new areas of open land, leading the way, preparing and improving the ground for other trees, shaping the landscapes they have occupied within their enormous geographical range. Birches are trees of superlatives: western Europe's most northerly growing species,[1] and in prehistory, the first to colonize the land at the heels of the retreating ice. A lump of birch tar thought to have been formed by our Neanderthal ancestors over 250,000 years ago may be the first synthetic product ever made,[2] and some of the world's oldest documents are written on birch bark.

Over time birches have created a vast reservoir of raw materials that have been immensely useful to mankind. All parts of these obliging trees – their leaves, twigs, branches and bark, as well as wood and sap – have given people of the northern forests the tools not simply to survive, but to flourish and express their identity in practical and spiritual ways with great sophistication. Tough, lightweight, watertight and flexible, birch bark has proved particularly versatile and useful, providing everything from housing and transport to food, clothing, footwear, musical instruments and medicines, as well as the means to communicate and to record sacred beliefs. In parts of Scandinavia, where bark was once a major export, bills and taxes could be paid with it; in northern North America birch bark defined an entire way of life. Because of the enormous mobility birch-bark canoes gave incoming traders and fur trappers, who travelled vast distances in these precision-built craft, exploiting Native American knowledge and skill, according to one specialist in native living skills, 'you could almost say the birch bark canoe built Canada.'[3]

Resources from birches have travelled far beyond their forest home to touch the lives of many of us, whether in the form of 'birch water', now available as a health drink around the world, chewing gum sweetened with sugar-free xylitol, a product worth hundreds of millions of dollars annually, birch plywood furniture or perhaps shampoo made with extracts from the leaves. Birches have long been used in traditional medicine, and research being carried out today into the array of useful chemicals they contain may yield powerful new medicines for the future to help us tackle some of our most serious ills.

As the national tree of Finland, Sweden and Russia, the silver birch is an important symbol of identity and national pride. Shortly after the death of Catherine the Great (1729–1796), peasant families of the Urals region who laboured on the reconstruction of the Trans-Siberian highway, which ran for thousands of kilometres to Moscow,

The distinctive indented leaves of *B. pendula* 'Dalecarlica', the Ornäs birch.

were ordered to plant and maintain an avenue of birch trees along some 160 km (100 mi.) of its length. The trees were not just national emblems, however, they had a practical purpose too: the silvery reflections of their trunks ensured that coachmen travelling this lonely route at night would not stray from the road.[4] Today, in Russia, the birch is a powerful symbol of the homeland and tradition as well as the representation of purity and light. Sweden's national tree is a silver birch variety (*Betula pendula* 'Dalecarlica') with deeply indented leaves known as the Ornäs birch (*Ornäsbjörk*), the original specimen of which was discovered on a farm at Lilla Ornäs, near Borlänge in central Sweden in 1767.[5] Declared the national tree in 1985, many Ornäs birches (distinguished by large crowns with branches that droop only at their ends), all derived from cuttings from this original tree, have now been planted in Swedish towns. *Björkarnas Stad*, 'the City of

Local people in traditional costumes carry a wreath decorated with birch leaves as part of the midsummer festival at Leksand, Sweden.

Birches', is the informal name for Umeå, considered the cultural centre of northern Sweden and European Culture Capital in 2014. The name dates back to 1888 when much of the city was destroyed in a catastrophic fire. Large numbers of birch trees were subsequently planted along the wide new avenues constructed to help act as fire breaks in case a similar disaster should occur again. In America's New Hampshire, meanwhile, the paper birch, found in all regions of the state and regarded as 'a characteristic part of the scenery', was declared the state tree in 1947.[6] In the *New Hampshire Troubador* (the state government booklet) it was also referred to as 'Queen of the Woods', a label that is part of a long history of association, certainly in Eurasia, with concepts of femininity and grace, something that features repeatedly in centuries of literature and art.

Practices originating in ancient symbolic associations still continue today. In parts of Scandinavia, as well as other regions of Europe and parts of Russia, the arrival of spring and summer are still celebrated with the help of birch. Green leafy branches – ancient symbols of new growth and fertility, also associated with the spirit world – are gathered to decorate maypoles or make garlands for people and animals, buildings and belongings. On Midsummer's Day in parts of Norway, even yachts and sailing boats may be festooned. In England, where the past presence and significance of birches is recorded in place names such as Berkhampstead, Birkenhead and Birkhall, their branches still decorate one Somerset church – St John the Baptist, Frome – at Whitsun. Silver and downy (*B. pubescens*) birches are familiar components of native British woodlands and heaths, but commercially grown hybrids of Asian and American species are now among the most popular and widely planted of ornamental trees in towns, gardens and parks.

While simply strolling through a birch grove is likely to reduce stress, silver birches, which are able to thrive in urban situations and have been found to be among 'the most ozone-tolerant' of central Europe's woody plants,[7] are helping us in more unexpected ways. Recent research has shown that, as street trees, birches are able to absorb more than 50 per cent of the particulate dust containing toxic

Silver birches outside houses in Lancaster, part of an experiment which has shown that these trees can absorb more than half the particulate matter generated by passing vehicles.

components generated by passing traffic.[8] After temporarily install-ing a row of young silver birch trees at the kerbside outside houses in Lancaster, and measuring the concentrations of particulate mat-ter found to be entering them (in comparison with that detected in homes without them), it was shown that the trees' leaves were remarkably efficient at filtering pollution and cleansing the air. Close examination revealed that they are able to trap pollution particles in the fine hairs and ridges on their surface. The 'open' arrangement of birch leaves and branches, so admired by artists and writers through-out the ages for its delicacy and for the dappled shade it casts, also assists with filtering, helping the air to circulate and flow past the leaves. Both practical and poetic, birch trees benefit us all.

one

The Natural History of Birches

Birches are members of the genus *Betula* and belong to the Betulaceae, a family of flowering plants that also includes hazels (*Corylus* spp.), hornbeams (*Carpinus* spp.) and alders (*Alnus* spp.), the genus to which the birches are most closely related. With a natural range that extends in a circle around the globe – across the cooler temperate regions of the northern hemisphere, from Britain and Scandinavia, through northern Russia, Siberia and northern China, to North America where they cover vast areas of Canada – they are found in a great range of habitats.

While the most southerly of the world's birches can be seen in the northern regions of Morocco, Thailand and Florida, this highly adaptable genus extends up to the frozen tundra of the Arctic Circle. Birches thrive both at sea level and in high mountain valleys, including those of the Alps, North Africa, the vast ranges of the Himalayas, the mountains of western China and those of Japan. They can be found too in the temperate rainforests of eastern Siberia and Korea, warm valleys in the Himalayan foothills, and subtropical forests that stretch from Nepal to Vietnam.[1] Here, *B. alnoides* (a Himalayan birch), becomes a lofty tree reaching some 30 m (98 ft) in height, whilst thousands of miles away the appropriately named dwarf birch (*B. nana*), adapted to survive the harsh conditions of the Arctic, is a small shrub that doesn't grow to more than a metre high.

Few other tree genera show such remarkable variety of form. Birch trunks may be slender or wide, single or multiple; crowns may be narrow, or broad and spreading. Leaf size and shape, colour and texture vary too, from the triangular double-toothed outline of the silver birch (*B. pendula*) to the almost circular or kidney-shaped leaf of the dwarf birch, which has distinctly rounded teeth. The translucent green of the downy or white birch (*B. pubescens*) in spring time contrasts with the leathery, dark blue-green of *B. szechuanica*, a subspecies

Birch trees in autumn.

Silver birches (*B. pendula*) in the Djebel Saghro mountain range, Souss-Massa-Drâa, southern Morocco.

of silver birch found in southwestern China and southeastern Tibet. Adaptation to particular habitats and environmental conditions in different parts of the world has resulted in enormous variation in outward appearance, not just between species of birch, but among particular groups of individuals of the same species. The paper birch (*B. papyrifera*), also known as the white or canoe birch, which extends

A birch, probably B. *pubescens*, covered in frost and snow on the tundra near Lovozero (Murmansk, northwest Russia).

from coast to coast across North America, and which is equally at home in oceanic conditions and the continental climate of the Rocky Mountains, is a good example: its leaves may be large or small, its mature bark white or brown, twigs and shoots very hairy or hairless with resinous 'warts'.

This lack of uniformity has helped make the identification and naming of birch species a particularly difficult job, which still continues. Estimates of the number of different species have varied greatly according to different methods used to assess them. Birches interbreed very easily and the large number of hybrids that exist, especially in cultivation, has added to the confusion, resulting in the incorrect or overlapping naming of many trees. In his foreword to *The Genus Betula: A Taxonomic Revision of Birches*, Lawrence Banks of Hergest Croft Gardens in Herefordshire has noted that 'the correct identification of birches has always been a lurking problem' and that 'there can never be a permanent definitive account of any genus as knowledge moves on.' The publication of this authoritative work, however, has provided 'a coherent and consistent classification of all the species of *Betula*, which has never been done before'.[2] The authors refer to 'the forty or fifty species of birch' currently thought to exist and 'accept 46 species' from the huge list of over nine hundred species and subspecies names that have at one time or another been applied to birches.

The book explains that three main groupings of what have appeared to be closely related species have 'remained more or less

Betula alnoides, a native of sub-tropical and tropical forests in northern India, Nepal, Myanmar, southern China, Thailand, Laos and Vietnam.

Dwarf birches (*B. glandulosa*) and willows (*Salix* spp.), in the tundra landscape of
Barrenlands, Central Northwestern Territories, Canada.

constant' during the attempts, over many years, to arrange them into groups: the white-barked birches, those found in the warm-temperate to subtropical forests of the Sino-Himalayan area and Japan, and the dwarf birches of the northern tundra and peaty swamps. As a result of their painstakingly detailed analysis and reassessment, Ashburner and McAllister have split the genus *Betula* into four subgenera, divided into eight 'sections', to which the various newly defined species and subspecies are allocated. At the most simple level, the birches that have white bark are separated from the 'thirty or so' that do not – loosely described as having brown or darker bark – and which also includes the group of seven dwarf birch species.

It is the white-barked birches, however, that are an especially complicated group and which taxonomists have had particular difficulty classifying. Common species such as the silver birch, downy birch, paper birch and *B. utilis*, which have a very wide and largely uninterrupted geographical spread, and which include trees that are significantly different at the extremes of each species' range, have

Birch forest in a Himalayan valley near Purano Mugu in mid-west Nepal.

proved especially troublesome as these differences occur as a result of continuous subtle variation, without the substantial breaks in distribution or appearance that might otherwise enable them to be split up into clearly separate species.[3] To make things more difficult, some dwarf tundra birches have hybridized with some of the white-barked species.

In the wild these trees are fast-growing pioneers 'designed to chase retreating glaciers and ice sheets'.[4] So successful are they at colonizing open land – quickly filling gaps in the vast conifer forests of the north and extending into the freezing tundra zone beyond, as well as the broadleaved deciduous forest to the south – that they have come to be regarded, unfairly, as 'weed' trees of the landscape.[5] In urban settings it's easy to see why this designation could also apply. Their preference for soils that are light, sandy and poor in nutrients (though they can cope with wet ground too), their relative drought-tolerance and shallow roots enable them (especially the silver and downy birches) to thrive on waste or abandoned land, such as derelict industrial sites, railway embankments and quarries, in dense groupings.

In his comprehensive treatise on trees, *Sylva*, first published in 1664, John Evelyn noted that the birch

> will thrive both in the dry, and the wet, Sand and Stony, Marshes and Bogs; the water-galls, and uliginous [swampy/muddy] parts of Forests that hardly bear any grass, do many times spontaneously produce it in abundance whether the place be high, or low, and nothing comes amiss to it.[6]

This tolerance of a range of soils and exposure, fast growth (producing a rapid effect in new planting and enabling birches to be grown as windbreaks) and medium size when mature, as well as the attractiveness of their bark and their relatively open canopy, which casts only a light shade, has made them ideally suited for moderate-sized gardens and public spaces in urban areas. The delicacy of their foliage

Birches growing in a bog in Upper Bavaria, Germany. Many birch species prefer permanently moist conditions.

in spring and good autumn colour are also important aspects of their appeal. Only a few of the white-barked species (chiefly silver birch, paper birch, wire or grey birch (*B. populifolia*) and *B. utilis*) are commonly cultivated, however.

Out in the countryside, the 'most influential members in the British landscape' are, according to some,[7] the silver birch and its close relative the downy birch, but the range of the silver birch extends far beyond Britain. In the wild, it is spread almost continuously throughout the boreal zone of northern Europe and Asia to Japan and across western North America. The outward differences that have evolved as a result of this enormous range have led to the classification of three separate subspecies.[8] One of these, found across Europe and eastwards towards central Asia, is subspecies *pendula* (formerly often

The distinctive trailing branches of the weeping silver birch, *B. pendula*, in early autumn.

An old German illustration of *B. pendula*, once classified as *B. verrucosa*, and referred to generally as the 'white birch'.

XVI. 5.

36. Betulaceae.

104. Betula verrucosa Ehrhart. Weiße Birke.

referred to as *B. verrucosa*, with reference to the sticky wart-like glands that develop on young shoots and twigs), the European silver or weeping birch, so named because of its characteristic 'weeping' branches. The European silver birch is unique in this respect: no other has branches that hang so elegantly, or particularly in older trees, vertically, and with its long-stalked leaves which flutter in the slightest breeze in summer, it's hardly surprising that these graceful trees are so well loved. Various cultivars have now been bred, selected for unusual variations of leaf colour or exaggerated weeping habit. Abundant in the wild in northern Europe, forming impressive stands and commonly occupying gaps in woodland, it has also become a distinctive feature of sandy heathland areas such as Germany's Lüneburg Heath. Here, in these man-made habitats, the silver birch, if left alone, will in time 'shade out' the heather (*Calluna vulgaris*) and replace it with birch forest.[9]

It is the downy birch, though (originally described by Linnaeus in his *Species Plantarum* (1753), along with the silver birch, as *B. alba*), that is the most widespread of the birches in Europe and western Asia. Although not found as far south, it has a similar distribution to the silver birch but tolerates colder, wetter habitats and grows further north than any other tree in western Europe.[10] Indeed, at Oksevåg on the Nordkyn peninsula at 71 degrees north, a small group of trees, said though to be *mainly* birch, some up to 6 m (19 ft) tall, has been designated 'the most northerly forest in Europe'.[11] Having evolved to survive in so many different habits, its outward appearance is very variable, with many regional forms able to reach 20 m (65 ft) in suitable conditions but less than 1 m (3 ft) in the harshest environments. A common feature, however, is the dense covering of fine, very short hairs on the young shoots, twigs and leaves – hence its Latin name *pubescens* – giving them a velvety feel. The small newly formed leaves of some populations emit a fragrant scent, particularly noticeable after summer rain, and from a considerable distance: 'As you approach the shores of Kamtschatka,' it was reported in the mid-nineteenth century, 'the birch trees send forth such a pleasant smell, that the sea-worn traveller suddenly imagines himself already on shore, inhaling the sweets of some fragrant grove.'[12]

The downy birch once largely covered what has now become Scotland's barren moorland of bracken, heather and grass. Along with the silver birch, however, these trees still form the country's commonest native woodland, also flourishing where protected from the predations of deer and sheep along stream banks or where the ground is too steep for them to reach. We shouldn't perhaps be surprised that the term 'birk' ('birch') is a common place-name prefix in Scotland, as elsewhere in the British Isles.[13] In the Scottish Highlands, birch woods

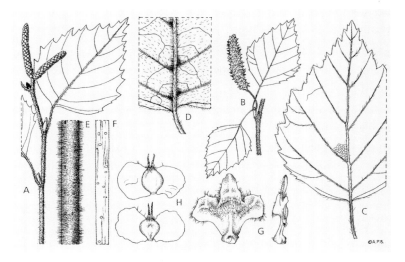

B. pubescens, var. *pubescens*, a twig with buds and immature male catkins (A); a fruiting shoot with mature fruiting catkin (B); the underside of a leaf (C); the underside of a very hairy leaf base (D); a densely hairy young twig (E); twig bark (F); female catkin scales (G); and seeds (H).

tend to lack fixed boundaries, the biology of the trees requiring that they 'have room to move around', invading moorland when browsing decreases and living usually 'for one generation of birchwood before dying out'.[14]

Tolerant of even colder temperatures, the dwarf birches *B. nana* – a low spreading shrub with densely hairy twigs – and the resin birch (*B. glandulosa*), which can be taller, are at home in mountain and sub-arctic moorland and in the icy conditions of the Arctic tundra. Here they form a significant part of the dwarf shrub community, often growing with dwarf species of willow (*Salix* spp.) and shrubs such as bilberry (*Vaccinium* spp.) and crowberry (*Empetrum nigrum*), though *B. nana* is also found much further south, in mountains including the Carpathians and the Alps. Distributed in different parts of the world, some dwarf birches such as the Japanese bog birch (*B. fruticosa*) prefer marshy ground, while another (*B. gmelinii*) inhabits sandy hills and deserts in Russia, Mongolia and elsewhere. By contrast, the group referred to as the brown-barked birches occur in the wild in areas of warm temperate and subtropical, species-rich, deciduous forest where they sometimes grow in pure stands, but are generally to be found as individual trees. Characterized by cherry or hornbeam-like leaves, as their name suggests they have barks that are dark, and at times almost black, often with a glossy, shiny or metallic sheen, or sometimes a white bloom. These brown-barked species are believed to look most like the ancient birches that existed during the prehistoric past. With little in common except features that were originally shared by all the birches,[15] and only distantly related to each other, they have proved difficult for botanists to put into groups.

Geological evidence tells us that birches are very ancient. Fossilized pollen resembling that produced by them and their closest relatives, the alders, has been found in rocks that are around 70 million years old.[16] Reproductive structures, including fruiting catkins and nutlets that are unique to birches, were discovered at One Mile Creek in British Columbia in deposits that formed around 50 million years ago,[17] showing that birches had become

Dwarf birch, *B. nana*, in autumn on the Saana fell above Kilpisjarvi Lake, Finland.

A birch-leaf fossil, some 50 million years old, discovered in Uintah County, Utah, USA.

clearly differentiated as a genus by that time. These discoveries have led experts to conclude that the genus *Betula* was in existence before the dinosaurs became extinct around 65.5 million years ago.[18] By this time trees belonging to the Betulaceae family had become widespread across what are thought to have been the warm, dry and relatively 'open' conifer forests of the northern hemisphere, extending across Eurasia and North America.

The oldest known fossil birch has been named *B. leopoldae*. The birch species alive today that is considered most similar to this ancestral birch is *B. insignis*, a large tree found in mountain forests in China.[19]

After 'the extinction event' that brought the Cretaceous era (130–65.5 MYA) to an end, the world's climate became generally

B. insignis twigs, one with upright female and long male catkins, produced in large showy clusters in spring.

warmer and wetter, with drier forest becoming rainforest in many areas, and with broader vegetation zones and much less seasonal difference. Fossil remains from the early Tertiary period that followed (65.5–23.03 MYA) suggest that while western Europe had a tropical climate at this time, on the most northerly land masses bordering the Arctic Ocean warm temperate polar forests existed in which birch-like trees were widespread. Gradually, genera, then subgeneric groupings, formed and as these became isolated by changes in geology and climate, different species evolved. The white-barked birches and the dwarf birches are thought to have evolved much more recently, not appearing in the fossil record until about 10 million years ago.[20] The birch species which grow today in our cold temperate and Arctic regions are thought to have developed their cold-tolerance on mountains further south and to have migrated north after the earth entered a period of climatic cooling, possibly some 3 million years ago.[21] Fossilized logs and leaves from Greenland show that the dwarf birch *B. nana*, along with other trees (such as pines, larches and yew) and plants, was growing in the northernmost Arctic before the Ice Ages of the Pleistocene Epoch began there about 1.8 million years ago.[22]

Of all the world's trees, it is the birches that are able to grow closest to the ice. Fossil pollen records show that during interglacial periods a birch zone existed, as it does today, between the deciduous forest in the warmer south and the tundra to the north. From this zone they both recolonized areas as the ice retreated and, as the climate grew colder again, spread out to dominate other areas before new ice sheets formed.[23] The dwarf tundra species *B. nana* (along with shrubby willow species and common juniper) is thought to have been present in the glacier-free part of southern Britain throughout the glaciations. Pollen evidence suggests that this and perhaps tree birches have been growing in the British Isles for the last 13,000 years.[24] As the last Ice Age came to an end it was birches, generally followed a little later by pines, that were the first trees to colonize Europe and form forests on their own. These birches then provided the conditions for other tree species, namely aspen and willow, to form with them what Oliver Rackham has termed the earliest 'wildwood'.[25]

Male catkins of the downy birch (*B. pubescens*) releasing a cloud of pollen grains.

The birches, then, are hardy pioneers. Staking a claim to freshly exposed soil and paving the way for other trees, they have evolved impressive strategies for survival. But how do they both benefit the wider environment and ensure success? Let's look at reproduction and growth first. The main way in which birches reproduce themselves in the wild is by the production of seeds. Birches are hermaphrodite and are mostly self-infertile. This means that separate male and female catkins are produced by the same tree – often on the same branch – but that they rely on pollen from other trees to fertilize them. The male catkins develop earlier than the female, and in tree birches lengthen considerably as they expand in spring. Creating a very impressive display, the longest, produced by *B. insignis*, can reach some 16 cm (6 in.). In contrast with most of the world's flowering plants, which depend on insects for pollination (and on birds and animals to disperse their seeds and fruit), birches rely on the wind to disperse the tiny pollen grains produced by the male catkins. Being carried by the wind enables the pollen, and therefore genetic diversity, to be exchanged over long distances. Whilst this is good news for birches, it's become bad news for humans: birch is now considered the most significant tree pollen to which people are allergic in the northern hemisphere, affecting between 5 and 54 per cent of the population of western Europe in the spring, depending on location (and causing reactions such as asthma, allergic rhinitis and conjunctivitis in locations as far apart as Europe, northern North America and Japan). The major culprit is the protein Bet v 1 to which an increasing number of people are becoming allergic.[26]

Once fertilized, each female catkin of the white-barked birches produces hundreds of minute seeds, with papery wings, only one-cell thick. After ripening, the catkins break up, allowing these seeds – over 11 million calculated for a single mature tree – to be picked up by the wind and dispersed.[27] Being generally lighter, smaller and spread over a wider area than the seeds of conifers such as pines and spruces, competitors among which they often grow, gives them a distinct advantage. Another big advantage over the conifers is that the faster-growing white-barked birches can produce seeds in just four years. Germinating and growing rapidly as long as there is strong light, seedlings will colonize any open land available, from heathland and clearances in woodland or plantations to disused quarries. In dense birch woods, however, it is hard for seedlings to become established, possibly due in part to shading but also because the roots of other birches are thought to secrete substances which deter competition.[28]

After quickly creating a network of fibrous roots that spread out from around the trunk to absorb nutrients and water and form a root plate to stabilize the tree, the larger roots take up minerals from deeper down in the soil. These minerals are effectively recycled as they are released back to the surface when leaves shed by the tree, which are slightly alkaline, rot down. The white-barked birches are known to improve the soil in this way, increasing its fertility, especially on acid heath land or in areas of former conifer forest, preparing it for other species which, given the opportunity, may replace them.[29] The trees don't work alone, however. Like those of other trees, birch roots have evolved a symbiotic relationship with particular fungi, the mycelium of which effectively become an extension of the birch's network of roots, helping obtain nutrients. At the seedling stage this is particularly important for the tree's growth. During their lifetimes birches develop an association with a large number of these fungi, most of them beneficial.[30] The toadstools commonly seen in the birch forests of the northern hemisphere in autumn, including the birch milkcap (*Lactarius tabidus*), birch brittlegill (*Russula betularum*), birch knight (*Tricholoma fulvum*) and the iconic fly agaric (*Amanita muscaria*) with its scarlet and white spotted cap, especially associated with mature birch trees, are the fruiting bodies of these mycorrhizal fungi. The dense clusters of twigs known as 'witches brooms', which look like birds' nests suspended in the branches of some birches, form owing to infection by ascomycete fungi.

Once established, birches have other tricks up their sleeves to help give them an advantage in their battle for survival. They are

Birch knight (*Tricholoma fulvum*) toadstools: one of the many species of fungi that develop a symbiotic root association with birches, it is common in Europe and in parts of the USA.

all, particularly the white-barked and dwarf species, able to tolerate exposure and are greatly helped in this respect by having leaves that are tough and mostly small – often smaller than those of other broad-leaved trees around them – and therefore less likely to get damaged. The young twigs and shoots of all birch species have hairs of one kind or another, though some are much more dense or prominent than others – perhaps a defence against the cold – and most have glands that produce resin, thought to possibly deter attack by aphids and the predations of herbivores.[31]

The beautifully varied, often peeling, papery and highly tactile bark of birches is perhaps their most distinctive feature and, for those that are cultivated, certainly responsible for much of their appeal. Colour and texture differ not just between species but between populations of the same species according to location, climatic factors and age. Hues range from brilliant white and subtle shades of cream, pink and yellow, through coppery orange and orange-red to all shades of brown and virtually black. Some barks are overlain with a misty

The striking white bark of the Himalayan birch, *Betula utilis* subsp. *jacquemontii*.

bloom, caused by the presence of betulin, a compound in the bark that makes it not only waterproof but highly resistant to decay and able to survive long after the wood of dead trees has rotted. Betulin and other chemicals found both in the bark and twigs is also thought to act as a form of defence against grazing animals such as deer, hares and rabbits tempted to eat the leaves and shoots of young birches, but not sheep (major inhibitors of the re-establishment of birch woodland on open ground in Britain).[32] In North America, porcupines and beavers are equally unaffected.[33]

The patterns of horizontal streaks formed by the lenticels (raised pores that allow gas to be exchanged between internal tissues and the air outside), which stand out in contrast to the bark behind, add to the attraction of birches and have become a distinctive feature of much artistic representation. But while attractive to us, the colour and remarkable texture of birch bark has clearly evolved for different purposes in nature. The whitest of the barks is perhaps that of a subspecies of silver birch, the Chinese white birch (*B. pendula* subsp. *szechuanica*), native to southwestern China and southeastern Tibet. Though tinged with brown or pale orange when young, the mature bark is an 'extraordinarily pure white', with cinnamon-coloured lenticels.[34] Unusually, though some other species do the same, this 'chalk-white' bark sheds large quantities of white dust. The purpose of this dust is not known, but a theory has arisen for the evolution of the white bark that protects birches in general. This is that the whiteness has evolved to reflect sunlight reaching it from its low angle in the northern sky, as a strategy to lessen the danger of the bark being overheated and scorched.[35]

The shedding of the outer bark in sheets and scrolls or small flakes, to reveal new layers of fresh and velvety or shiny bark beneath, is a curious phenomenon performed by members of certain species in distinctive ways. In some, such as *B. utilis*, widely cultivated in Europe and North America, bark varies from the striking white of subspecies *jacquemontii* (native to the Kashmir region) to copper, or darker shades in other subspecies, and is shed in large and spectacular sheets or scrolls. In others, such as *B. dahurica* from eastern Asia, a great number of small curling flakes give a distinctively shaggy appearance. The slow-growing yellow birch (*B. alleghaniensis*) of eastern North America is unique for its metallic yellowish-bronze bark that also peels in curling shreds and strips.

It is fascinating to speculate about why such strategies or adaptations should have evolved. An intriguing theory has been put forward by environmentalist and author George Monbiot, to explain the evolution of what he describes as 'the pied coat' of the European silver birch.[36] With reference to the 'megafauna', including straight-tusked elephants, that roamed across Europe until hunted to extinction around 40,000 years ago, Monbiot suggests that the birch's bark, which in old age becomes 'corrugated like the cracked surface of a lava flow',[37] could in fact have evolved as a form of 'elephant-proofing' since 'the black fissures make the white skin harder to strip cleanly'. He goes on to explain:

> Our ecosystems are the spectral image of another age, which, on evolution's timescale, is still close. The trees continue to

arm themselves against threats which no longer exist, just as we still possess the psychological armoury required to live among monsters.[38]

Birches are certainly survivors, but the white-barked birches that are most commonly cultivated are, in general, relatively short lived, typically reaching in the case of B. *pendula* only some sixty to eighty years. Lifespan

The spectacular orange-brown peeling bark of a Himalayan birch (B. *utilis*) near Namche Bazaar, Khumbu, Nepal.

The metallic glinting bark, shed in curling flakes, of the yellow birch, *B. alleghaniensis*, native to North America.

Birch bark that has become corrugated and cracked with age, resembling a lava flow.

will depend very much on growing conditions: the more unfavourable, the more slowly the tree will grow and the longer its life will usually be. In southeast Greenland a stem of B. *nana* has been recorded with 147 growth rings, leading some to surmise that this species may be the longest-lived of all the birches.[39] It is also reported, however, that the paper birch, generally reaching 100–140 years, may live for over two hundred years,[40] and that slower-growing species such as the yellow birch, which often forms an important component of old growth forest, can exceed three hundred years.[41] But when is a tree's life really at an end? Young birches can sprout up from the base of a trunk when it loses vigour and also from the stumps that remain after cutting or other damage, caused for example by fire – something which most of the conifers with which they compete are unable to do.

However long they live, birches are important for wildlife. From a total of some 499 species of insect and mite that feed on these trees in Europe, some 133 depend on them exclusively.[42] A total of 344 species are estimated to feed on the silver birch and downy birch in Britain alone.[43] These include the caterpillar of the small tortoiseshell butterfly (*Aglais urticae*) and those of many moths, including the buff tip (*Phalera bucephala*), the pebble hook-tip (*Drepana falcataria*), the Kentish glory (*Endromis versicolora*) and the angle shades (*Phologophora meticulosa*).[44] Birch seeds, meanwhile, are an important food for a variety of birds, especially finches, including redpolls (*Acanthis* spp.) and siskins (*Spinus* spp.), which have bills that are specially adapted to feed on birch and alder catkins, and they feature in the diet of a number

Kentish glory moth (*Endromis versicolora*), whose larvae feed on birch and alder.

of others including the goldfinch (*Carduelis* and *Spinus* spp.), bullfinch (*Pyrrhula pyrrhula*), greenfinch (*Chloris chloris*) and serin (*Serinus serinus*), the smallest of the European finches. They are also eaten by members of the tit family, such as blue tit (*Cyanistes caeruleus*), great tit (*Parus major*) and chickadee (*Poecile* spp.). Larger birds, such as the ruffed grouse (*Bonasa umbellus*) and ptarmigan (*Lagopus* spp.), eat birch buds and seeds too, including those of dwarf birches (*B. glandulosa* and *B. nana*). In the Highlands of Scotland, some 28 species of bird depend on the habitat provided by birch woods.[45] Various mammals, including voles, shrews and mice, eat the seeds of, or live in close association with, birches. Deer and moose consume large numbers of birch seedlings, as well as woody stems and leaves. In order to get to its nutritious inner layers, they cause considerable damage by stripping bark from the trees – an activity shared, in the USA, with the snowshoe hare, beavers, porcupines and squirrels.[46]

Many plants too, including juniper (*Juniperus communis*), wild cherry (*Prunus avium*), bird cherry (*Prunus padus*) and redcurrant (*Ribes rubrum*), are associated with the birches that extend across Eurasia.[47] While hole-nesting birds make use of dead or decaying trunks, across

A redpoll extracting seeds from birch catkins.

Common in the
northern and eastern
USA, yellow-bellied
sapsuckers return
frequently to the
holes they have
drilled to extract
sap, as well as the
insects that are
attracted to it.

Canada, Alaska and northeastern North America, the aptly named
yellow-bellied sapsucker woodpecker (*Sphyrapicus varius*) drills tiny
closely spaced holes in the bark of healthy trees and drinks the sap
that trickles out.[48] But it's not just birds that have learned to make
the most of this phenomenon.

Trees in early spring, as the sap begins to rise, in Chernigiv, northern Ukraine.

two
Tree of Well-being

A s winter comes to an end, new life stirs and a process of
transformation begins. The lengthening days and warming
of the soil send vital signals to the birch. The tree begins
to turn starch stored over winter into sugars, and developing root
hairs increase its ability to take up water from the ground. Water is
pulled into the tree, carrying sugar and minerals up to the dormant
branches. When a branch is broken or cut, or the bark damaged, the
rising sap, a clear, colourless liquid retaining, as John Evelyn put it,
'an obscure smack both of the taste and odor of the Tree', flows out.[1]
People across a vast area of the northern hemisphere, from Britain,
France and Scandinavia in the west, through Poland and Slovakia
south towards Romania, and across the former Soviet Union to
northern China, Korea and Japan as well as northern North America,
have been making use of this phenomenon since time immemorial
by tapping and drinking the sap from the trees.[2] With their huge
geographical ranges, this includes for example the silver and downy
birches across Eurasia, as well as B. costata in the Russian Far East, and
in North America the silver birch, paper birch, the cherry or sweet
birch (B. lenta), the yellow birch, the black birch (B. nigra) and the river
or water birch (B. occidentalis).

Over a thousand years ago in 921 CE, Ahmad ibn Fadlan, an Arab
traveller, recorded the use of fermented birch sap by the Turkish-
speaking Bolgar people of the Volga river in Russia,[3] and there is a
long tradition of drinking the fresh sap in Europe and elsewhere:

Sap drips from a tube inserted into a birch in Ukraine, where it has been drunk by locals since time immemorial.

a fourteenth-century medieval document recorded the Norwegian King Sverre and his men as having 'spent two nights in the wilderness with no food but sap they could suck from the trees'.[4] Another from the same period recorded the Siberian Uriankhai people drinking the sap 'instead of water'.[5] In North America birch sap has long been enjoyed, as a food and medicine, by woodland Indians from the northeastern USA across Canada to Alaska: the sap of the yellow birch, for example, drunk by Algonquin and Iroquois tribes, sometimes mixed with maple sap.[6] Appreciated in northern and eastern Europe and beyond not only by ethnic peoples, forest workers and herdsmen but by those living in urban areas, and by rich and poor alike, the sap, commonly collected throughout forested regions, was taken to nearby towns in barrels to sell. During the eighteenth to nineteenth centuries birch sap sold at Transylvanian markets was an important source of income for local people.[7]

The sap can only be collected during a short period, however, depending on location and weather conditions, from some ten days to about three weeks (usually from around the middle of March to the beginning of April) before leaves are produced by the trees in early spring. This period coincides with the 'hungry gap', the traditional time of food deficiency before agricultural crops are ready for harvest, which was still a feature of life in northern Europe until the end of the nineteenth century and until the 1960s in eastern Europe. In the forested or semi-forested regions where other sources of water were hard to find, it's not hard to see why the sap should have become important. With a subtle, slightly sweet taste and containing a range of minerals (varying greatly depending on where the trees grow), including potassium, calcium, magnesium, manganese and zinc, vitamins C and B group, antioxidants, amino acids and sugars,[8] it was a welcome relief after the long northern winter, providing not just a refreshing drink, but an important source of nutrients. Fresh sap cannot be kept for long, however: some suggest that, cooled or refrigerated, it can last for a maximum of five to six days; others say two weeks. If not refrigerated, fermentation begins after two to three days. Commonly drunk fresh with lemon juice or other plant extracts, traditional methods of preserving it are the making of fermented drinks, chiefly ale and wine, and sometimes vinegar, and also reducing it to a sweet syrup. With the addition of grains, dried fruit, chunks of rye bread, flour, yeast or malt, in many countries an ale similar to the famous eastern European *kvass* (a fermented drink of the Baltic and Slavic region) has been made – often flavoured with other plants including bog myrtle (*Myrica gale*) or juniper (*Juniperus communis*) – and saved for drinking in the summer, during hay-making or the cereal harvest. In North America, especially in the northeastern USA and Newfoundland in Canada, 'birch beer' has come to mean something rather different. Originally involving the boiling of bark and fermentation with yeast, today, unless made at home, it is a carbonated soft drink, of which many different brands are available, flavoured with birch or other extracts.

Russia, Estonia, Britain, Latvia and Scandinavia, among other regions, have a long history of birch wine production and in Sweden today, a sparkling wine, Sav, is being made from a recipe dating back to 1785. Spirits such as vodka and, more recently, gin may also include birch sap or extracts from the buds as a flavouring.[9] Another product with a long history of use, like birch sap itself, which is now finding a new commercial popularity, is birch syrup. Unlike the much sweeter maple sap containing mainly sucrose, birch sap can contain from around 1 to 2.6 per cent sugars depending on the species of birch, its location and the weather conditions at the time of tapping.[10] The main naturally occurring sugar is fructose (said to be more easily digested than sucrose), followed by glucose, a small amount of sucrose and traces of galactose. Birch syrup, traditionally obtained by boiling the sap to evaporate off the water, has long been used as a sweetener by Native Americans and in Eurasia as a sugar substitute, especially during wartime.

In Scotland, where birch trees are being tapped once again in the traditional way[11] the sweet syrup used to be reduced further to make a 'sweetmeat'.[12] By far the biggest commercial producer of syrup today is Alaska, where vast mixed birch and spruce forests carpet the interior and south-central parts of the country, and where the largest producer now collects sap from between eleven to sixteen thousand paper birch trees each year. After treatment by reverse osmosis, which removes 70 per cent of the water, the sap is evaporated to a con-centration of 67 per cent sugar. Some 455 l (100 gallons) of sap are needed to make 4.5 l (1 gallon) of birch syrup.[13] With a distinctive flavour resembling caramel or molasses, described as more savoury than sweet, the syrup is a versatile product that blends with and enriches other flavours.

Birch sap is usually collected by drilling a hole or making a slit in the trunk – generally at between 30–60 cm (1–2 ft) and 1.5 m (5 ft) from the ground – and then inserting something for the sap to flow along by surface tension (a twig, a grooved peg or V-shaped piece of metal or wood), or through, such as a wooden spout or length of plastic or metal tubing (a hollow elder stem or funnel made from birch bark were sometimes used in the past) into a container, typically a large plastic bag or drum attached beneath. Sap can also be collected

Icelandic liqueur made from distilled grain spirit infused with birch buds, with the addition of birch syrup.

from fresh birch stumps, by making a hollow in them. John Evelyn's *Sylva* (1664) discussed various aspects of tapping, including the relative merits of the type and position of incision to be made, and which side of the tree was best: he recommended facing southwest.[14] In his *Vinetum Britannicum*, a treatise written in 1676 on a range of drinks that could be made from fruit in Britain, however, John Worlidge, also describing the collection of sap in England, advised that

> many Gallons in a day may be gathered from the Boughs of the Tree by cutting them off, leaving their ends fit to go into the mouths of the Bottles, and so by hanging many

Workers gather plastic sacks containing birch sap near Minsk, Belarus.

Bottles on several Boughs, the Liquor will distil into them
very plentifully.

Sap was best tapped, he said, from the branches, 'having had a longer
time in the Tree, and thereby better digested and acquiring more of
its flavour, than if it had been extracted from the Trunk'.[15]

What an individual tree will yield each day varies enormously
depending on its size, location and weather conditions (more sap is
generally produced in wet, cool conditions), but an average for the
silver and downy birches in Russia is in the region of 4–5 l (7–9
pints) per day.[16] The 'Korean' birch (B. costata) is generally regarded
as the most productive – a single tree is said to have the capacity to
produce some 50–78 l (90–140 pints) daily.[17] Opinions have varied
about the appropriate quantity to extract to avoid the exhaustion of
individual trees. Commercial collectors in Alaska today give each tree
a two-year rest between tappings. Some may wait longer. If done in
moderation, tapping is said not to injure the tree and holes are generally plugged at the end of the season to stop infection from entering,
though there is some debate about the usefulness of this practice.

The antiquity of sap collection and its significance to the peoples of the northern hemisphere is reflected by terms such as *сакавік* ('birch sap month'), the name for March in Belarus, and similar terms traditionally used in Finland, Estonia and Latvia for April, *berezen*, or *березень*, in Ukraine and *březen* in the Czech Republic (both translatable as 'month of birches'). Here, this important event was widely celebrated with festivities which included the drinking of the fresh sap by girls which would, it was believed, help them grow into healthy, fertile women.[18] The idea that birch sap imparted vitality was very prevalent. There is a long history in eastern and northern Europe (including the Russian Arctic) of adults and children drinking it as a general tonic, and in Romania it was given to weak children to strengthen them. Various other saps were also collected, including maple (*Acer* spp.), beech (*Fagus sylvestris*), ash (*Fraxinus excelsior*) and lime (*Tilia* spp.), though birch was the most significant. It has been suggested that the consumption of tree saps was one of the most important and effective means of protecting against scurvy in former times.[19]

Men carrying buckets of sap collected in forest areas isolated from sources of environmental pollution, Ukraine.

But the drinking of birch water, as it was also known, has been considered useful for a range of medical conditions and claims concerning its properties are very old: German, Italian and Swedish medical texts dating back to the sixteenth century all refer to it. The Italian botanist and physician Pietro Mattioli (1501–1577), for example, stated that it could be used to cure ulcers and also kidney and gall stones.[20] This claim was echoed by the English herbalist, physician and astrologer Nicholas Culpepper (1616–1654), who wrote in his *Complete Herbal*, 'The water that comes from the tree being bored with an auger . . . is available to break the stone in the kidneys and bladder and also good to wash sore mouths.'[21]

Birch wine, too, was considered medicinal. John Evelyn, writing in *Sylva* in 1664, reported that it was very beneficial for 'curing . . . Consumptions, and such interiour diseases as accompany the Stone in the Bladder or Reins [kidneys]'. He reproduced a recipe sent to him by 'a fair Lady', which he said could do 'wonders for cure of the Pthisick'.[22] European and Russian folk medicine repeat these claims,

Carton of birch sap (referred to as water) tapped from trees in Finland.

especially the alleged capacity to flush out toxins, and also include the treatment of liver, stomach and lung problems, chilblains and colds, gout, hepatitis, bronchitis, intestinal worms, pneumonia, headaches, jaundice, conjunctivitis, constipation, earache, rheumatism and arthritis, and use as a diuretic. The sap was thought to be beneficial for animals too, and has had a number of veterinary uses, including increasing milk production in cattle.

Largely promoted as a detoxifying, low-calorie health drink, 'a natural anti-inflammatory diuretic that helps the liver detoxify chemicals and the kidney expel uric acid from the body', with vitamins, and minerals and a quarter of the calories of coconut water, the niche marketing and promotion of 'birch water' outside countries of traditional consumption has become big business today.[23] One British company website claims that it 'is also useful as a part of herbal therapy for the treatment of osteoarthritis as it acts on the inflammation of synovial ligaments, tendons and the contraction of muscles'. Furthermore, it claims, drinking the sap 'improves skin conditions which are the result of the accumulation of waste products due to disorders of the excretory systems'.[24]

The belief that birch sap is good for the skin, inside and out, has long been held in eastern Europe and Russia. A pale skin was especially prized during the nineteenth century, and birch water was considered to be effective as a face wash to lighten and 'beautify' the complexion and in particular to remove or diminish freckles. In Estonia the first few drops of sap tapped in spring were thought to keep the skin fair all summer. Sore eyes might also be treated with a compress of birch or maple sap.[25] Recent research has suggested the beneficial effect of sap on the moisture retentiveness and barrier function of human skin cells,[26] and experiments with extracts of silver birch leaves have suggested a skin-lightening effect.[27] Sap has also been widely recommended and used for washing the hair and commonly regarded as a stimulant, able to prevent baldness and promote hair growth. In parts of Bulgaria it is considered effective if rubbed onto the roots of the hair for this purpose.[28] In central Italy, added to a decoction of the bark, it has been a traditional treatment for alopecia.[29] Perhaps its most famous advocate, Queen Victoria, is reported to have drunk 'large quantities' of birch sap when she was at Balmoral Castle, 'in an attempt to halt the thinning of her hair'.[30] Birch sap has been incorporated into various cosmetics and toiletries, including perfume and shampoo, for many years, and with its new popularity its use looks set to rise.

Until the collapse of the Soviet Union in 1991, the centralized collection of birch sap, begun in the 1920s, was undertaken on an industrial scale. By the late 1980s production had exceeded 70,000 tons per year. Sap was very cheap and always available, even when there were shortages of many food items. But its consumption fell drastically following the Chernobyl nuclear disaster in 1986 and the resulting fear of contamination, Chernobyl being located in the main birch sap region of Ukraine (the major producer in the days of the Soviet Union). Russia, Ukraine, Belarus, Estonia, Latvia and Lithuania have continued to be producers both for commercial sale

Female catkins of the bog birch (*B. pumila*), native to North America. One of the dwarf birches, it favours swamps and wetlands.

and domestic use. In Ukraine, for example, where birch sap is very popular, the start of the tapping period is still an important event each year, announced in newspapers and online, with films demonstrating collection techniques as well as recipes for its use,[31] and birch sap festivals are also held.[32] Recent years have seen a revival of interest in its use in a number of other traditional collector countries, for example in Scandinavia and Canada. Much of the sap collected commercially from numerous small-scale harvesters in countries such as Finland, Latvia and Ukraine is exported frozen to companies around the world, then filtered and pasteurized before being bottled, with citric acid added as an antioxidant.

It's not just the sap that has been used as a medicinal aid across Eurasia and North America: so too have the catkins, buds, leaves, twigs, roots and bark. Tinctures or decoctions of the buds and leaves of silver and downy birches are recorded in the folk medicine of Russia and a number of European countries from Portugal in the west to Greece, the Balkan region and Lebanon in the east, and extending beyond into central Asia for many of the maladies treated with sap.[33] A traditional treatment that seems to have been particularly widespread – practised in the past by the Inari Sami of Finland and reported from Lebanon and parts of Transylvania, where it still continues – is the use of birch leaves for rheumatism and arthritis. This involves the patient lying for some hours on a bed of young 'resinous' birch leaves or, for painful legs, wearing trousers or a sack filled with them to cause heavy sweating.[34]

Birch fruiting catkins (sometimes referred to as cones) were chewed by the Sami or made into a tea to help treat coughs, while the Ojibwe of Canada inhaled the aromatic smoke produced by heating them to treat catarrh.[35] Native American peoples also made medicinal use of the twigs, roots and bark of various species, including the yellow birch – the source of a fragrant oil used to flavour other medicines – and the sweet birch for a number of different complaints. Both these species contain the compound methyl salicylate, also known as oil of wintergreen. The bark and wood of the sweet birch, distinguished by the strong, minty smell of the twigs and shoots when scraped, were formerly used for the extraction by distillation of oil of wintergreen (Pennsylvania being noted for its production as long ago as 1882),[36] a substance now made commercially by chemical synthesis. Birch bark is particularly significant with regard to its numerous traditional medicinal uses (many overlapping with those of the leaves and sap) and the potential of some of the chemical compounds it contains. While strips of bark were burnt by Native Americans in tepees used to heal the sick, so that the smoke would cleanse or purify the air, bark decoctions, with reputed analgesic and fever-reducing properties, have been widely drunk in northern and eastern Europe and elsewhere for fevers and colds, and in the past in Russia for the treatment of malaria. Birch bark has also been applied externally for skin diseases and sores and for the healing of wounds.[37] In northern India and Nepal the papery bark of B. *utilis* has been placed directly onto wounds and burns, and a paste of boiled bark of this or another Himalayan birch, B. *alnoides*, applied to help heal swellings, microfractures and dislocated bones.[38] Boiled and pounded birch bark was used in a similar way by Native Americans as a poultice for wounds and, after soaking in water to soften it, to make effective casts or splints which became rigid once dry. Cataracts could be removed with tiny bark slivers.[39] The Yakut people of Siberia traditionally made bandaging from heated birch-bark strips,[40] while in Transylvania prisoners captured during the Second World War treated their wounds with bark as an anti-inflammatory.[41]

Leaf or bark extracts (sometimes referred to as *Betula alba*, the name originally given to both the silver and the downy birches by Linnaeus in his *Species Plantarum*, 1753) are incorporated into various contemporary Western herbal preparations commercially available today, as well as homeopathic treatments. However, one particular product obtained from the bark (though also present in the wood) stands out. This is birch tar, a kind of pitch, also referred to in its most liquid form as birch oil – a thick, syrupy, dark brown substance, looking not unlike used motor oil. It is obtained by pyrolysis – effectively 'baking'

Oil extracted from the bark of the cherry or sweet birch (*B. lenta*) has long been used in folk medicine.

birch bark in airless conditions at temperatures between 250° and 400°C (480° and 740°F), in a sealed container or oven-like structure (which can be formed from earth or sand, or other materials) with a fire around it, and which allows the pungent, viscous liquid produced to be contained separately by dripping into a container placed below it. Although it will eventually harden and set, by boiling this oil it slowly thickens and on cooling begins to solidify. The process must be carefully carried out as the tar can easily burn and turn to carbon. Taking different forms according to temperature, once solidified it can be heated again to produce a liquid, acquiring a putty-like consistency of various degrees of stickiness and malleability in between. Hugely useful as a waterproof glue and sealant, it has been put to numerous highly practical uses (see Chapter Three) that stretch back into the prehistoric past.

With regard to medicine, birch tar has achieved a distinctive status and been hailed as 'a remedy against 100 diseases'[42] with, it is claimed, antiseptic, disinfectant, pain-relieving and fever-reducing

Birch bark coiled inside a bucket in preparation for being heated to produce birch tar.

properties, among others. Archaeological evidence has shown that the use of birch tar is extremely old and that it may well have been used as a 'masticant medicine' for many thousands of years. What may be the earliest finds, from the Upper Valdarno Valley in Italy, are thought to possibly date back to an astonishing 250,000–260,000 years BCE.[43] Small amounts of birch tar have also been confirmed on 82 artefacts found in Germany's Inde Valley, which date to around 120,000 years ago. Such archaeological evidence, going back to the Middle Palaeolithic, a time generally regarded as the epoch of the

Neanderthals, alongside reconstructive experimentation, have led some to conclude that birch tar may be the 'first synthetic product' ever made by humans, demonstrating not only control of fire, but a process of 'complex cognition'.[44]

It seems that our Neolithic ancestors may have been making birch tar regularly. An oblong lump of tar from Königsaue in Germany, almost fifty thousand years old, shows evidence of kneading, but finds of tar in bog sites in Germany, Scandinavia and elsewhere in northern Europe, dating from the early Mesolithic (some nine thousand years ago) with clearly defined teeth marks, have indicated that birch tar was also chewed. Finds from Bökeberg in southern Sweden suggest that another prehistoric chewing gum, pine resin, was also in use at around this time.[45] Since the tooth impressions on these ancient birch tar finds have led to the conclusion that many of the chewers were children aged between six and fifteen, it is thought that such chewing might have been done to help remove loose milk teeth, or perhaps simply for soothing purposes.[46] However, much more recent

Liquid birch tar has a wide range of uses including medicine, fuel, glue, waterproofing and the preservation of leather and other materials.

use made of both birch bark and tar by the Inari Sami indicates that it may have been done to release compounds (with antimicrobial activity) to help disinfect the teeth and gums, or to treat dental or other problems, such as a sore throat (a condition also treated in Nepal by chewing bark) or cough. The Sami have traditionally chewed birch bark to ease coughs and keep their teeth and gums in good condition, and either chewed or rubbed a lump of birch tar or pine pitch on a

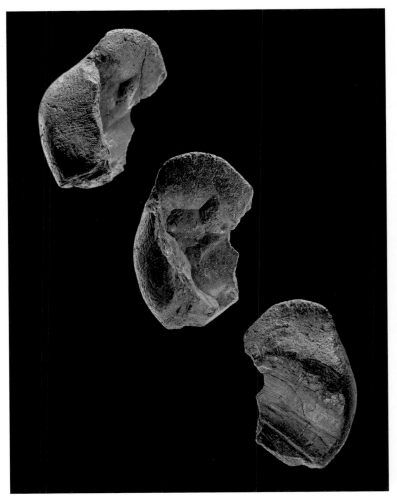

Pieces of prehistoric birch tar from Königsaue, Saxony-Anhalt, Germany.

painful tooth. A further fascinating traditional practice employed by them for toothache was warming up a chrysalis found on birch branches in winter, taking out the larvae and pressing it into a tooth cavity, thereby, no doubt, making use of the compounds absorbed by the insect from the tree.[47]

Highly valued in the folk medicine of northeastern Europe and Russia, birch tar has also been used in veterinary practice as a vermifuge and to protect people and their domestic animals from mosquitoes and other biting insects. For disease protection and to deter insect pests, a tar solution was sprayed onto crop plants as well as the ground. Horses' hooves and buildings for livestock were also treated with it. In Russia smoke produced by dropping birch tar onto red-hot embers was also considered a means of disinfecting houses.[48] The Sami, meanwhile, breathed in the steam created by tipping tar water onto hot stones to treat coughs, and drank a 'tar water' made from pine or birch tar to treat rheumatism. They also used the tar to close wounds.

Birch tar is particularly associated with the treatment of conditions and diseases affecting the skin, such as eczema, psoriasis, scabies, some forms of dermatitis and fungal infections, as well as wounds, sores, ulcers and burns. During the Second World War an ointment containing birch tar, Vishnevsky liniment, was widely used for these purposes and is still made. Exported largely from Russia, Lithuania and Ukraine, many other birch-tar products are commercially available today for the treatment of skin conditions, including oil, soap, shower gel and shampoo. These commonly state that birch tar stimulates the regeneration of the epidermis and that it has an anti-inflammatory and anti-pruritic effect. Research suggests that tars, including birch tar, can inhibit the excessive production of skin cells by temporarily affecting the production of DNA,[49] promoting a return to normal skin development – something that is important for sufferers of conditions such as psoriasis, in which excessive skin deposition is a problem.[50] In laboratory tests using extracts of the bark of the yellow birch and Japanese or Alaskan white birch (B. *pendula* subsp. *mandshurica*) similar effects have been observed on psoriasis- and dermatitis-like disorders in mice, as well as a decrease in skin irritation.[51] The salicylates (salicylic acid and methyl salicylate) in birch tar, which act as exfoliators, help remove dead skin.

While there has been some concern about the safety of the prolonged use of birch and other tars on the skin, with reference, for example, to an increased risk of skin cancer, it has been concluded by some that 'despite the extensive use of medicinal tars, particularly in psoriasis patients, there is no epidemiological evidence that topical tar products . . . cause cutaneous or internal cancer'.[52] Indeed, it seems with regard to a number of their chemical components, that the opposite may be true: they may able to help prevent or treat cancers.

Russian anti-dandruff shampoo containing birch tar.

A packet of betulin,
extracted to 95 per
cent purity from
birch bark.

Containing a cocktail of useful chemicals, some of the bio-compounds
found in birch tar and birch bark have been the focus of much recent
scientific research, not only providing an explanation (at least in part)
for some of the trees' traditional medicinal uses, but offering the
prospect of a source of new medicines to help us fight some of our
most difficult medical battles. Of particular interest are those belonging to a group of triterpenoids, especially betulin, the substance that
gives the white-barked birches their distinctive white appearance
and which can comprise around 30 per cent of the dry weight of their
bark, and betulinic acid, present in much smaller quantities but easily
derived from betulin, with a wide spectrum of biological activity.[53]

Laboratory experiments suggest that these compounds have
impressive anti-cancer capacity, particularly when modified to increase
their water-solubility.[54] They are able to inhibit the migration and

kill the cells of certain strains of a number of different types of tumour, including those of breast, lung, colon, prostate and skin cancer, as well as leukaemia, neuroblastoma, myeloma and glioma, and cancers of the ovaries, cervix and thyroid, while being non-toxic to normal human cells.[55] Other attributes include antibacterial, antifungal, antimalarial, antihelmintic, antioxidant and anti-inflammatory activity – this last supporting another common use of birch in traditional medicine for the treatment of inflammatory diseases such as arthritis. Clinical tests on animals, using leaf and bark extracts of the silver birch and its subspecies the Japanese white birch, have indicated anti-inflammatory activity that may be helpful for sufferers of rheumatoid arthritis as well as inhibition of cartilage degradation that occurs in osteoarthritis. Liver- and stomach-protective activity is also reported.[56] Of great interest too is their antiviral potential, having shown activity against the herpes simplex, Epstein-Barr and hepatitis C viruses, with betulinic acid and its derivatives having indicated particular anti-HIV activity.[57] Recent research has suggested, furthermore, that betulin (a valuable precursor of biologically more active compounds) can decrease the production of cholesterol and fatty acids, reduce diet-induced obesity and help the body to regulate the production of insulin. Because it has been found to stabilize and reduce the size of fatty deposits in blood vessels, it has been proposed as a treatment for metabolic diseases including type 2 diabetes.[58]

With regard to the skin, bark extracts, especially those with a high percentage of betulin, have been shown to have skin-barrier reinforcing properties and been assessed as potentially helpful for dealing with dryness.[59] A number of cosmetic products and toiletries incorporate betulin or betulinic acid and derivatives of the latter are reported to be potentially useful for the prevention of damage from UV light. Somewhat ironically, birch bark is currently regarded as a low-value waste product in the forest industry with no economically significant use. The extraction of betulin, only small amounts of which are currently available, and other chemicals including suberin (a waxy organic compound) on an industrial scale from this waste has, however, been suggested in order to provide a large, low-cost supply, not only for the manufacture of pharmaceutical compounds for medicines and cosmetics, but for a range of industrial and agricultural applications. It has been estimated that a pulp mill producing some 200,000 tonnes of birch pulp a year creates enough bark waste for around 4,000 tonnes of betulin to be extracted.[60]

Birch trees share some of their chemicals with other forms of life that depend on them. Betulinic acid is to be found, alongside an impressive array of other compounds, in the remarkable polypore fungus *Inonotus obliquus*, a white rot fungus commonly known as *chaga* (a name thought to be probably derived from the Old Slavonic term *gaga*, for 'lip'),[61] found growing almost exclusively on birch (though occasionally on alder and beech) trunks in the very cold forests of the northern hemisphere. Its peculiar, gnarled appearance, an irregular, blackened, cracked and encrusted tumour-like growth with a hard outer surface, has given rise to names such as 'cinder conk', 'clinker polypore' and, in Norway, *krefikjuke*, or 'cancer polypore' (known also as *shulta* in Siberia). The blackened appearance of the dense, woody mycelium, the vegetative part of this parasitic fungus, which erupts through the bark of the tree, is due to the large amount of melanin present. Inside, the fungus has a yellow-brown corky consistency, with a marbling of cream-coloured veins. Growing only very slowly, but able to reach considerable size – up to 40 cm (16 in.) in diameter – and able to re-grow after removal, it eventually kills the host tree some twenty years or so after first infecting it, its fruiting body later releasing its spores before it, too, dies. Extracts in water have been widely used for many centuries in folk medicines as a general panacea, certainly across Russia where the fungus is still very popular, northern Europe, and parts of Asia, including China, for a range of maladies including stomach and intestinal problems (such as ulcers and gastritis), tuberculosis, for various skin diseases and to alleviate hunger, tiredness and pain.[62]

The Khanty and other Siberian peoples, including the Nenets, Komy, Selkup, Evenki, Even and Yakut, have traditionally drunk a *chaga*

Inonotus obliquus, or *chaga*, growing out of a birch trunk in Marquette, USA.

tea for general well-being and the prevention or treatment of various illnesses, and prepared a water for washing and disinfecting the body with the fungus after heating it like charcoal. Like the Ainu people of Sahkhalin and Hokkaido, they have traditionally smoked powdered *chaga* for ritual cleansing purposes. It is perhaps best known, however, for its long use (recorded since the early sixteenth century) for the treatment of cancers in Russia and northern Europe without toxic side-effects.[63] *Chaga* is famously mentioned in Alexander Solzhenitsyn's semi-autobiographical novel *Cancer Ward* by the central character Oleg Kostoglotov who, while suffering from cancer, 'could not imagine any greater joy than to go away into the woods for months on end, to break off this "chaga", crumble it, boil it up on a campfire, drink it and get well like an animal'. The novel also mentions an old country doctor, Sergei Maslennikov, who had observed that:

there was no cancer among the peasants who came to him
. . . and instead of tea [they] brewed up a thing called 'chaga'

or in other words, birch fungus . . . Mightn't it be that same 'chaga' that had cured the Russian peasants of cancer for centuries without their even knowing it?[64]

Solzhenitsyn, who won the Nobel Prize in Literature in 1970, had been a patient on a cancer ward in a clinic in Tashkent, Uzbekistan, after years in a Stalinist labour camp. He is reported to have been amazed at the effectiveness of the fungus, which it is thought he probably took himself to help treat his own malignant tumour.

Having acquired almost legendary status as a medicinal aid and more recently as a fashionable 'super food' supplement, a vast body of scientific literature has been looking at *chaga*'s chemical make-up. Extracts vary in their chemical constituents, depending on how they have been produced and where the *chaga* was grown, but laboratory research indicates that compounds such as lanosterol, inotodiol and ergosterol[65] can indeed inhibit the growth of some primary and secondary tumours, in particular during the early stages, both by selectively killing affected cells without damaging host cells and by stimulating the body's own defences. It seems that they can strengthen the immune system to help the body not only deal with the harsh effects of chemotherapy and radiation treatments – relieving pain and improving the appetite – but inhibit diseases caused by viruses including strains of influenza and HIV. Antioxidant and anti-inflammatory properties have also been identified, as well as others that may help prevent mutagenic diseases.[66]

Traditionally consumed by crumbling or grating to a powder and then boiling to make a tea (the hot water extracting compounds held within the hard chitin cell walls), it is claimed that the *chaga* with the greatest therapeutic potency is found on trees that have endured the harshest environmental conditions, experiencing UV irradiation and periodically freezing temperatures (in some parts of Siberia reaching -50°C (-58°F)), and that its medicinally active compounds possibly develop as a result of this and the fungus's struggle to overcome the defence systems of its host birch tree. Certainly, attempts to cultivate it by fermentation show that without the tree only some of its bioactive substances can be produced.[67] A large market has developed, with great demand from Asian countries, supplying the Internet trade and health food shops and offering *chaga* preparations of many kinds. Large quantities are reported to have been collected from the forests of Siberia.[68]

It isn't just the *chaga* fungus that is of medicinal interest. Another kind of polypore, *Fomitopsis betulina*, the birch polypore or birch bracket fungus, so closely associated with the birch that it has defined its scientific and two of its common names, has a very distinguished, exceedingly ancient claim to fame. Minute investigation of everything found with him revealed that Ötzi, the famous iceman murdered in the Ötzal Alps, on the Italian/Austrian border, some 5,300 years ago, carried with him two small pieces of birch polypore, threaded onto thongs made from strips of animal hide, one with an elaborate three-lobed tassel.[69] Detailed research to determine his state of health when he died revealed that Ötzi was infected with whipworm (*Trichuris trichiuria*), since eggs of this irritating internal parasite were found in his digestive tract. It is thought that he may have been carrying the fungus in order to treat this infestation, since it contains, among other things, polyporenic acid, which is effective at killing whipworm.[70] It was reported that some of the compounds in the fungus were possibly 'the only remedy available in Europe' during Neolithic times to fight this parasite.[71] The fungus is said to still be in use for this purpose today in Poland and Italy.[72] Ötzi's stomach was infected with *Helicobacter pylori* bacteria too, which can cause chronic gastritis and other stomach problems, including peptic ulcers and stomach cancer. Again, the birch polypore, reported to have been traditionally used in Bohemia to treat stomach problems and rectal cancer, may have been helpful, since research has suggested that compounds it contains (including betulinic acid) may have anti-cancer as well as antiviral, anti-inflammatory and antimicrobial properties. Indeed it has been reported that among ten species of polypore tested against eighteen bacterial strains, *Fomitopsis betulina* was 'the most active'.[73] The

Two pieces of birch polypore *Fomitopsis betulina*, found with Ötzi the Iceman (a 5,300-year-old glacier mummy) in the South Tyrol in 1991.

effects of a tea made from this fungus have been described as anti-fatiguing and soothing.[74]

Better known to some as the 'razor strop' because of its former use for this purpose by surgeons and barbers (among a number of other intriguingly varied uses), the fungus also has a styptic effect and, cut into small strips, could be applied like a plaster or bandage. As well as the many smaller cuts that Ötzi incurred just a few days before he died, he had a deep, unhealed cut on his right hand. Although it couldn't have stopped him bleeding to death from the wound inflicted by the arrow that severed one of his arteries, perhaps this fungus was used to help treat his more minor injuries.

In a small pouch stitched to a leather belt, Ötzi was also found to be carrying, alongside various flint and bone tools, material from another bracket fungus: the tinder fungus *Fomes fomentarius*, found in the northern hemisphere, most commonly on birch trees. Known to have been used for thousands of years in its whole dried form as a means of transporting fire (something that can also be done with dried *Fomitopsis betulina*, which also smoulders very slowly), and in prepared form as *amadou*, a pre-eminent tinder for fire-lighting, it had other fascinating uses, including the making of clothing. Known

Fomes fomentarius, a tough bracket fungus on an old birch tree in the Craigellachie National Nature Reserve, Scotland.

also as the hoof polypore because of the shape it assumes as it grows, it could be used, like the birch polypore, for medicinal purposes. Worked by hand to form a wad-like consistency, it has a long history of use as a styptic and as an absorbent dressing for wounds and burns. In what would appear to be something of a contradiction, it could be used for cauterization, by lighting and applying it, as it was smouldering, direct to the skin nearest the affected part or organ to cure pain. Experts have concluded that fire-making was probably the use Ötzi made of this fungus.

Polypore fungi have featured in the cosmological or spiritual beliefs of native peoples in many parts of the world. Considered to have a spirit power and to be magically protective, pieces of polypore were incorporated by Native American Plains Indians within the medicine bundles used by their shamans, attached to sacred clothing, and worn as necklaces to protect against illness.[75] Since the birch polypore and tinder fungus grow mostly on birch trees, which are considered in much European and Siberian mythology to be sacred, it seems possible that Ötzi carried these fungi for spiritual as well as highly practical medicinal purposes – important components perhaps of a Neolithic survival kit.

Birch trees have a much more recent connection with health care. The timber of some of the white-barked species is a significant source of xylitol, a white, crystalline substance that dissolves in water and is as sweet as sucrose but with some 40 per cent fewer calories.[76] With a cool, fresh sensation when eaten, it is widely used today around the world and promoted for use in oral health care, as well as in dietary and other food products, in pharmaceuticals, cosmetics and toiletries (as a humectant or skin conditioner) and as a sugar substitute for diabetics.[77] Most xylitol is destined for chewing gum, a use expected to account for about 163,000 metric tons by 2020, with a value of just over U.S.\$1 billion.[78] This substance (a carbohydrate, actually a sugar alcohol) is made by our bodies in the course of their metabolism every day, but it occurs widely in low concentrations in many vegetables and fruits, though in quantities too small to make commercial extraction viable. It is obtained by chemically processing woody, fibrous plant matter that is rich in a specific starting material, xylan. Cereal crops such as wheat, oats, rice and maize (corn) are all xylan-rich but so are certain hardwood trees, in particular birch and beech. Corn cobs and wood pulp are the major raw materials for xylitol production today. Making use of the 'waste stream' derived from the pulping of wood for fibres, paper production and other products, around 95 per cent of the pulp used currently by Dupont, the largest producer of xylitol in Europe, is made from birch trees, with other hardwood species forming the rest. The birches are said to be sourced mainly from forests in Austria, with additional timber coming from Germany, the Czech Republic, Slovakia, Hungary and other parts of the EU. In the USA wood pulp used by this same company is mostly derived from birch but also maple species.[79]

After 'cooking' the wood chips with magnesium bisulphite at about 150°C (302°F) to break them down, the raw pulp is separated, leaving a waste product also known as 'black liquor'. It is from this that xylose, a 'wood sugar', is extracted and converted to xylitol (technically, a 'poly-alcohol' or 'polyol') by catalytic hydrogenation (a process that turns the sugar into an alcohol), before being purified by crystallization.

Xylitol was first identified in a syrupy substance extracted by research chemists in Germany from beech wood chips, and in France from wheat and oat straw in the late nineteenth century. A process of purification had been discovered by the 1930s, but it wasn't until the period of the Second World War that a shortage of sugar in various countries, including Finland with its vast birch forests, encouraged the search for alternative sweeteners. An industrial process for xylitol production was then developed there. This paved the way for its later development as a commercial sweetener.

After the war years, it was the potential of xylitol as a medical tool that initially began to be exploited and until the 1970s, when research into its uses in dentistry was first carried out in Finland, it was used mostly in producer countries (especially Germany, the USSR and in Japan) as a diabetic sweetener and for intravenous feeding.[80] With a very low glycaemic index compared with glucose and absorbed only slowly by the body, independently of insulin, it doesn't cause a rapid increase in blood sugar. Large-scale production of xylitol began in Finland in 1975, the year in which the first chewing gum containing it was made. Studies carried out in the 1970s looked at its effect on dental plaque in comparison with other sugars.[81] Significantly, unlike sucrose and various other sweeteners, xylitol resists fermentation and can't be used as an energy source by cavity-causing bacteria in the mouth. This suggested that its usage could lead to a significant reduction in dental decay. It was also suggested that, consumed regularly, it could assist the remineralization of layers of enamel. As a consequence, xylitol has been much promoted commercially, especially for long-term use as a preventative of tooth decay and for the reduction of plaque formation.

Its real effectiveness has become a controversial issue, however. Various studies conclude that the claims concerning remineralization are not proven.[82] Some suggest that xylitol may not be any better than other polyols like sorbitol or only equal to fluoride in preventing cavities, and that any cavity-reducing effect may be due not to xylitol but to the simple process of chewing and its consequent stimulation of saliva, which helps neutralize the acidic environment created by microorganisms in the mouth.[83]

Whatever the truth, since xylitol can also be produced by microbial processes involving bacteria, fungi and yeasts, such biotechnological approaches to its production may one day consign this use of birch trees to the past.

John Everett Millais, *Winter Fuel*, 1873, oil on canvas.

three

Practical Birch:
Materials for Life

E very part of the birch has been of use to people and just about every part continues to be used today. In the cold, wet forests of the north, it must have been an invaluable discovery that birch bark will burn so readily. The high proportion of oil it contains means that it is one of the best natural tinders to get other fuels burning. A small piece of the outer bark, removed from the tree, then scraped and roughened with a blade to create fine shreds and increase the surface area, takes a spark very readily, even when wet, and burns hot and fast. Today's survivalists and woodsmen, such as British expert Ray Mears, who have learned so much from old traditions, value the birch highly for this purpose, regarding fire-making as 'the number one use of the bark in the bush'.[1]

In England during the Middle Ages, Northumberland fishermen, or 'Fisherers' as William Turner called them in his *A New Herball* of 1551, burned strips of birch bark wedged into 'the clyft of a sticke' to attract fish to their spears at night,[2] a practice also employed by Native American woodland peoples. The clear flame produced by lighting folded bark that had been placed in poles some 1.5 to 2 m (5 to 6 ft) long, positioned at the head of their canoes, illuminated night-time fishing expeditions. Various kinds of birch bark torch were also made: the Gitksan and Wet'suwet'en of the conifer-forested landscape of northwestern British Columbia, for example, and the Ojibwe (also known as the Chippewa, one of the group of culturally related Anishinaabe peoples of Canada and the northeastern USA)

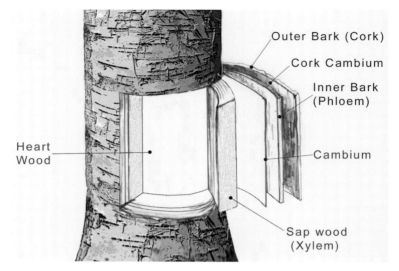

Outer Bark (Cork)

Cork Cambium

Inner Bark
(Phloem)

Heart
Wood

Cambium

Sap wood
(Xylem)

A trunk section showing bark layers.

twisted pieces of bark into rolls or horn-shaped cylinders, some of which would burn all night.[3] In Scotland, meanwhile, and in other parts of northern Europe, birch bark was twisted into a 'rope-like form' and used in place of candles.[4]

But bark – this fantastically versatile, multi-purpose material – has enabled peoples who have lived among birch trees across a huge geographical region to do so much more; from travelling at speed on water to creating waterproof homes and making essential items of all kinds, from baskets and containers to tools and equipment, clothing, musical instruments, forms of communication and food. The structure of birch bark is largely responsible for the secret of its success. In very simple terms and for practical purposes, a distinction is made between the 'outer' bark, also referred to as the cork, and the 'inner' bark. Each year, the cork cambium, a thin layer of cells on the inner surface of the cork, produces a new layer of outer bark, the oldest part of which begins to peel off naturally as the tree ages and expands. On the other side of the cork cambium is the inner bark, or phloem, which distributes the products of photosynthesis from the leaves to the other parts of the tree and which makes up some 75 per cent of the total bark. This is produced in layers by the vascular cambium which separates it from the xylem or sapwood beneath, which it also produces and which carries water and nutrients from the soil to the leaves.

At the right time of year, and with the right technique, the outer bark can be removed from a living tree relatively easily, but the procedure must be carried out very carefully in order to not damage the inner bark and possibly kill the tree. Cylinders of bark can also, or course, be removed from sections of a felled tree or a decaying log. Bark can be stored for many years, either in flat sheets or rolled bundles, but may need soaking or heating before use, though narrow strips may not need such treatment. The outer bark can generally be split into thinner, more flexible layers. It is these layers, containing high levels of betulin and the water-repellent compound suberin, which together confer particular decay-resistance, that have proved so very versatile. Baskets and containers of all kinds have been made from birch bark for thousands of years. Ötzi the Iceman was carrying two. With sides formed from cylindrical sections of bark, their round bases were stitched in place using bast fibre from lime trees. One held Norway maple (*Acer platanoídes*) leaves that had been freshly picked, and small pieces of charcoal. It is thought that, wrapped like this, Ötzi would have been able to carry the embers for some hours, fanning them alight when needed. Birch bark containers, which are extremely light and strong, are still being made in the Italian province of Trentino near the site of Ötzi's discovery, having survived for at least five thousand years as a traditional local craft.[5]

In Scandinavia, where the roots of birches have also been used for basketry, the use of birch bark has similarly ancient origins. The Bronze Age Egtved Girl, who was buried in Norway nearly 3,500 years ago, though thought to have been born in southwest Germany, was found with a round birch bark container holding bronze pins, a sewing awl and hairnet by her head. Another, which had once held a kind of beer (made from wheat, honey, bog myrtle and crowberries), had been placed at her feet.[6] During the eighteenth and nineteenth centuries the use of bark boxes for snuff as well as tea, coffee, tobacco, salt and butter were popular in Scandinavia, a major advantage being that they did not transmit any taste and retained moisture, while also keeping unwanted moisture out. Many boxes or baskets for these uses have been made by folding bark into the desired shape and holding it in place with wooden pegs, and/or by stitching with roots. In northwest Siberia, Selkup, Nenets and Khanty women still collect and sew bark to form baskets of this kind. Sealed bark containers holding the afterbirths of female children were traditionally hung from birch trees in the hope that Khanty girls would become skilled users of bark.[7] In other parts of Russia too, and across the birch-forested regions of northern and eastern Europe, birch bark is still widely used.

Native Americans of the boreal and subarctic zones are renowned for the extensive use they have traditionally made of this and other

One of the two birch bark containers found with Ötzi the Iceman on the Italian/Austrian border.

A Selkup woman removes bark from a birch tree near Bistrinka in Western Siberia to make a traditional basket.

barks (including elm, hemlock and cedar) and in particular that of the paper birch, forming a significant part of the material culture of a number of tribes. Lightweight, flexible and strong, an enormous variety of household items from simple trays and dishes, ladles and spoons, to storage boxes, drinking cups, buckets and cooking pots have been produced for a multitude of purposes, from the winnowing of wild rice and the carrying or keeping of foods (including beans, berries, corn, meat, animal grease and fish) to the storage of goods for ceremonial and medicinal use. Those made by Anishinaabe peoples, who have traditionally lived in the Upper Great Lakes area and who continue to produce *makakoon*, are particularly well known. Typically decorated with beads or porcupine quills, sometimes applied with the help of patterns or stencils (made from fine bark sheets bitten to form precise indentations), these are containers, with rims often reinforced with wooden splints or grass, made by heating bark and ingeniously folding it into shape (with the outer bark on the inside) before piercing and sewing with *watap* cordage. Flexible and strong, *watap* has been traditionally made from plant fibres, especially the

An etched birch bark basket, made *c.* 1890 in Maine, USA, by Sabattis Tomah, Passamaquody cultural leader.

roots of various conifers such as spruce or cedar, which have been de-barked and soaked, then steamed or boiled to make them pliable. *Makakoon* were so well made that liquids such as birch sap and syrup and soluble items such as maple sugar, used both as a sweetener and seasoning, could be kept in them. Tiny cone-shaped containers filled with solid sugar might be suspended from a baby's cradleboard, while large bark funnels were used for jobs such as pouring hot fat into bladders for storage. Some, sealed with pitch or resin and completely waterproof, were used to cook food, hung carefully over a fire so that their contents could be heated without the container igniting. Another cooking method was to place hot rocks in a bark container that held water, which would then cook the food placed in it.

Alaskan Athabaskan peoples have similarly used bark, collected in spring or early summer when soft and malleable, to make an assortment of baskets for gathering, preparing or storing foods. As noticed by ethnographers observing its use in various parts of the world including Russia, 'a peculiarity of the bark is that it keeps from decay whatever is stored in it' – its chemical compounds have a preservative effect.[8] Meat, fish and berries, for example, might be placed in a bark container with a lid folded over and tied or sewn shut and placed in a cold store underground.[9] In British Columbia and elsewhere layers of bark that were as fine as tissue paper but extremely strong and durable were used to wrap foods, and underground pits were lined and covered with birch bark to keep food in good condition for long periods of time. A similar practice has been traditional in western Nepal with the bark of *Betula utilis* for preserving food grains.[10]

With its antibacterial and antifungal compounds, birch tar offered the preservative qualities of birch bark in more concentrated form. Neolithic pottery finds in northern Greece show that the tar was used some seven thousand years ago to line the interior of jugs with low porosity – that is, they didn't need this lining to make them waterproof.[11] In Russia fermented drinks were once commonly stored

'Flower Field' created by Pat Bruderer of the Cree nation, one of the last practitioners of the complex art of birch bark biting.

in containers or wineskins that had been treated with birch tar, not only conserving them but giving them a distinctly smoky flavour.

Birch bark has not just helped to preserve food and drinks but has been eaten as a food too – not the outer bark but the cork-like, reddish inner bark or phloem, the specialized cells of which store starch and allow water and nutrients to be distributed throughout the tree in spring. The American anthropologist Frank Gouldsmith Speck, writing in the early twentieth century about the Montagnais (today, the Innu) of the Labrador Peninsula and Quebec, noted that 'The inner bark of the canoe birch . . . is grated and eaten as beneficial to the diet at times.'[12] The Cree and Chipewyan of Saskatchewan also ate the bark and it was a significant enough practice to give rise to the name by which another group of Algonquian peoples formerly living near modern-day Montreal in Canada came to be known: the Adirondack. This name, thought to have been first used in the late 1500s, is derived from an expression used by the Mohawks, an Iroquoian people, translated as 'they eat trees'. It was said that this was a reference to the Algonquian custom of eating tree bark when other food was scarce.[13] Harvested during the spring, when low in fibre but high in sugars, it was a seasonal food. The inner bark of large trees was said to be sweetest and could be eaten fresh – favoured by children as a treat – or dried and ground into flour. Edible inner bark from a number of shrubs and trees was once a significant seasonal source of carbohydrate for various Native American peoples.[14]

To the west, across the Bering Sea in Kamchatka, birch bark was reported in the early nineteenth century to have been cut into strips 'like vermicelli' and dried for eating later, and elsewhere to have been 'reduced to a powder' and 'beaten up with the ova of the sturgeon'.[15]

Birch bark has certainly been eaten since ancient times in Scandinavia. The Sami, for whom the inner bark of the Scots pine (*Pinus sylvestris*) was once a staple food, ate birch bark too.[16] Said to have a nutritional composition of 1,000–1,200 calories per kg, bark flour was used to supplement grain flour elsewhere in Scandinavia during the eighteenth and early nineteenth centuries, when bad harvests caused serious food shortages. During his travels, Carl Linnaeus is said to have noted with concern 'the dire situation of forests which could not survive the widespread debarkation that peasants' need for the bark flour resulted in'.[17] In combination with rye or wheat flour, bread incorporating a small percentage of bark flour is now being prepared again in Sweden in some specialized bakeries.

If not providing food directly, bark and its product, tar, have played a part in making some of the equipment used to obtain it. Highly effective as a glue and sealant, perhaps the most distinguished ancient use of birch tar is in the weapons and tools used by Ötzi during the Copper Age (a period of the Late Neolithic that marked the beginning of the Bronze Age). Both the flints that formed the tips of his wooden arrows and the very valuable copper blade of his axe (the only one of its kind ever found) were fixed into their shafts with birch tar, the axe blade also being tightly bound with leather straps and the arrowheads with plant fibres to keep them in place. The fletching at the ends of the arrows was also glued with birch tar and plant fibres. Rich in tannins and containing betulin, it was important not just as a glue but as a very effective preservative, once widely applied to

Flour produced by grinding dried inner birch bark.

81

The flint tips of Ötzi´s arrows and the copper blade of his axe were partly held in place and the joins sealed with birch tar.

Ötzi's axe.

prevent the decay of wooden structures of all kinds, from cartwheel axles, fences and boats to houses, and also to preserve fishing nets and ropes. Birch-tar oil, also known as 'Russian petroleum' since it was used as a fuel too, was issued to the British Army for use as rifle oil before the First World War.[18]

Birch bark, meanwhile, was skilfully turned by Native Americans into bark quivers for bows, while protective arm guards for archers could be fashioned by wrapping a bark section around the forearm. Rolled into a conical tube it could amplify the imitation of moose, deer or bird calls to attract them for hunting. Canadian birch bark moose callers said to 'really . . . make a difference' can be bought today on the Internet.[19] In Europe, meanwhile, birch bark played a significant role in the construction of similar horn- or trumpet-like instruments, particularly by herdsmen until the turn of the twentieth century, across most of the mountainous regions of Europe, from Scandinavia and the Alps to the Carpathian Mountains. Commonly used to call or herd grazing animals in mountain pastures and to scare off bears and wolves, they were also used to communicate messages over long distances, and mark collective events in the pastoral and religious year, evolving into musical instruments along the way.

Melodies created on them by herdsmen and women, played from memory and improvised upon over generations, were to form or play an important part in the development of regional and national folk music traditions. They also influenced the compositions of at least two classical composers, Johannes Brahms and Jean Sibelius,[20] and the use of many such instruments has continued or been revived today. With a history of use stretching back into the distant past, the simplest were made from rolls of bark, such as the *tuohitrumpetti* (bark trumpet), *kuoriklarinetti* (bark clarinet) and *parkkipilli* or *tuohihuilu* (bark pipe) played in Finland.[21] Others relied on bark as a binding around lengths of hollowed wood. The *trembita*, for example, which can be 3 m (9.8 ft) in length, traditionally used by shepherds in the Carpathian region of Ukraine, Poland, Slovakia and Romania, and which

A traditional birch bark moose caller, sewn with spruce roots, made in Quebec by Hank Rogers, an Algonquin artist.

could send announcements such as deaths, funerals and weddings across a distance of over 10 km (6.2 mi.), is still heard in Ukrainian folk music and featured in the winning song of the 2004 Eurovision Song Contest.[22] In Switzerland the long tradition of playing the *büchel* (a type of alpine horn with a wind tube resembling that of a trombone or bugle) also continues, though its birch bark binding has been replaced today with a rattan strip. In Norway the traditional herding instrument the *lur* or *neverlur* (described in Icelandic sagas as a war instrument to frighten the enemy and marshal troops) is still made and played,[23] as is the similar *näverlure* of Sweden.[24] In Finland, meanwhile, the *toropílli*, a traditional instrument of the Karelian region (on the Finnish/Russian border) used by cattle herders, resembling a clarinet in structure and with tightly bound birch bark at the end of the instrument forming a cone to amplify the sound, and other instruments incorporating birch bark are being used once more by Finnish musicians today.[25] A surprising reinvention of the birch bark rattle, used as long ago as the Middle Ages in Finland, is the woven birch bark *rapaball* – a contemporary percussion instrument which can be used acoustically or with an inner microphone to create an impressive range of sounds.[26]

The *trembíta,* a type of wooden alpenhorn bound together with birch bark, is a traditional instrument of the Hutsul people of the Carpathian mountains.

Bark rattles for ceremonial use were a feature of Native American life, as well as fans designed for different purposes, from fanning fires and cleaning living spaces to helping ward off illness or cure the sick. Decorative fans, often ornamented with feathers, indicated the status or the family to which the carrier belonged. Those used in dancing and in purifying rituals and medicine ceremonies had important spiritual significance. The Ojibwe hung thin strips of bark outside their wigwams so that their snake-like undulations when the wind blew would frighten away the unwanted spirits of the dead.[27] The unique properties of birch bark have made it suitable for articles of clothing too, including the distinctive pointed hats decorated with feathers or tufts of animal hair at the point worn by the Abenaki of the northeast woodland region. There is evidence of birch hats being worn in Europe too. Excavation of the richly furnished burial mound of what is thought to have been a Celtic chieftain in Baden-Württemberg in Germany, dating from 530 BCE, revealed a man wearing, among other things, a birch bark hat. Some 1,300 years later, conical but flat-topped birch bark hats covered with cloth or animal

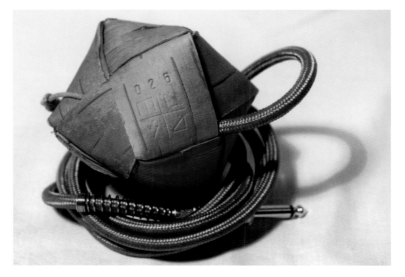

A contemporary percussion instrument created in Finland by Juhanna Nyrhinen, the hand-woven birch bark *rapaball* is an electrified shaker.

A hand-coloured engraving (c. 1820) of a Mari woman, wearing a birch bark hat.

skin and embellished with shells, beads and coins still formed part of the distinctive costume of Mari (formerly known as Cheremis) women from the Volga-Ural region of Russia.[28]

As protection from the wet, this lightweight material was invaluable and many northern cultures made use of its waterproofing capacity. Its use in hats worn in the nineteenth century in Europe and presumably by colonists in North America was noted by John Loudon, the Scottish botanist, garden and cemetery designer, author and editor, who recorded in his *Arboretum et Fruticetum Britannicum*

(The Trees and Shrubs of Britain), that in Maine, in Canada, thin strips of bark from the paper birch were placed in the crown of hats as 'a defence against humidity', in a similar fashion he said to 'the bark of the birch of Europe . . . in Lapland'.[29] In former times Sami people shaped pieces of bark to form light yet weatherproof clothing, worn like a cape around the shoulders. They too, along with a number of other peoples, made boots or leggings of birch bark, which was also worn inside shoes to keep out the rain.

In Norway, where the right to harvest birch bark was to become encoded in law, the practice of wrapping birch bark around the legs to keep them dry was the origin of the name *Birkebeinerne*, literally 'birch legs' (now generally referred to as Birkebeiners), used it is said originally as a form of insult for people considered so poor they couldn't afford shoes. The name was adopted by one of what were to become two main factions (the other being the Baglers) who claimed political power, and the right to choose succession to the throne during the period of civil war from 1130–1240. After the death of King Håkon

Knud Larsen Bergslien, *The Birkebeiners Skiing Across the Mountains with the Royal Child*, 1869.

Sverresson, his immediate successor Håkon Håkonsson, whose life was endangered by the Baglers, was taken by the Birkebeiners at the age of eighteen months on a treacherous journey by ski from Lillehammer through the mountains to safety in Trondheim. He was no doubt carried in a birch bark wrapping or backpack of some sort, this being a traditional way of transporting and cradling children where birch forests abound. Today the rescue of Håkon Håkonsson is commemorated in Norway by annual sporting events: a cross-country run, a mountain bike race, a cross-country ski race and a road cycle race. Those competing in the bike and ski events must carry a backpack weighing at least 3.5 kg (7.7 lb), symbolizing the weight of the child the Birkebeiners had to carry on their journey. Cross-country ski races are also held in the USA, Canada and Australia.[30]

As a form of eye protection from the snow, strips of birch bark with slits cut just wide enough for the wearer to see through or with semicircles cut out and bent down could be worn to prevent snow blindness. Shoes made by weaving strips of the brown inner bark or 'bast' layer, had become the standard footwear for the poor by medieval times in northern and eastern European countries,[31] including Finland, Poland, Lithuania, Latvia, Estonia, and in the Ukraine, Belarus and Russia, where they were still commonly worn in the twentieth century. Different types of shoes were made for different types of terrain – some with lower sides, better suited to walking across boggy areas, a benefit being that water could drain through them easily, while others could be stuffed with hay or other materials to help keep the feet warm. Known as *lapti* in Russia, they were commonly worn with a strip of cloth wound around the foot and lower leg, held in place with laces of twisted birch, elm or lime bark. (As with Birkebeiner, the term *lapti* came to be used as an insult.) In rural Finland women made many pairs of such shoes each year to provide footwear for their families. Tough, durable, fast drying, cheap and quick to make, it is not surprising that they were so popular. A pair was said to last for some 16 km (about 10 miles) of continuous walking before needing repair – a distance referred to as the 'birch bark mile'.[32] They are still being made and used in various countries today, including Finland and Russia. In the Tomsk region of western Siberia, where there has been a revival of interest in the creation of traditional and some very new birch bark products, from jewellery to passport covers, and where a 'Golden Birch Bark Festival' is now held, bark shoes and inner soles are proving popular. Though reported to be less durable than those made of lime bark, they are said to be comfortable and to have therapeutic value, since it is claimed the compounds they contain cure 'skin diseases and old sores'.[33]

The preservative properties of birch tar – long used by Slavic peoples to treat clothing – helped create a Russian export that came to achieve great fame because of its unique qualities: Russia leather. Combining outstanding durability, suppleness and resistance to water, this high-quality leather with its distinctive smell was highly sought after in particular for footwear, such as the tall boots or *sapogi* used by the nobility and army officers. During the seventeenth and eighteenth centuries it became an important Russian export. In order to make it, hide (calf skin for the best quality) was tanned by steeping for several weeks in a solution of inner birch bark (an important traditional tanning material and source of a yellow-brown dye in various parts of the world), though spruce and willow were also used. In a process that distinguished it from the processing of other kinds of leather, birch tar oil was then carefully rubbed into the flesh side of the hide and allowed to soak in and saturate it fully.

As a specialist craft carried out in only a small number of villages, the way in which the tar used in the complex and lengthy curing process was obtained and the difficulty of reproducing it outside Russia played a large part in the mystique that surrounded the product elsewhere. During the nineteenth century production of Russia leather slowly moved to other countries, but the birch tar or oil needed still had to be imported from Russia or Poland. Though other oils might be used, none had the distinctive aroma of the traditional birch, considered an indicator of quality. Dyed red or black and often 'tooled' for decorative effect, different kinds of Russia leather were made

A pair of contemporary Finnish birch bark shoes (*virsus*) made by Eero Kovanen.

for different purposes. One of these was the upholstering of chairs, when such luxury items first began to be common, in the seventeenth century – particularly approved of in Britain by the Puritans during the Interregnum period (1649–60). Fixed in place by distinctive, large-headed brass nails, only Russia leather was flexible and strong enough to be stretched for chair use without cracking and maintain its strength. Since volumes bound in it were able to resist attack both by the mould and insect activity that afflicted others, the binding of books was another major use. A consignment of Russia leather discovered by divers in 1973 on the sea floor beneath the wreck of the *Metta Catharina*, a Danish ship that sank in 1786 off Plymouth Sound in England, is still being used to make leather items, including shoes, in London. The remarkable preservation of these reindeer hides is due not only to the thick mud which concealed them, but to their careful preparation and the extraordinary properties of the birch oil treatment they received over two hundred years ago.[34]

Just as bark provided clothing for daily life, it also accompanied the dead. The deceased might be wrapped in it or placed in birch

A modern key ring from George Cleverley & Co Ltd., London, using Russia leather dating from 1786.

bark coffins, a practice undertaken by Native Americans such as the Ojibwe and Iroquois, in Siberia and probably elsewhere. The same enduring qualities that helped protect and initiate the journey of the dead were put to outstanding use for the living in the form of the birch bark canoe. Known to have been used for many thousands of years, these highly versatile, lightweight craft were masterpieces of design. With a birch bark hull, supported by a wooden frame, lashed together with spruce or other roots, their construction reflected their makers' detailed and intimate knowledge both of their environment and the properties of the raw materials it supplied. Built in different sizes and for different purposes, from the one-man fishing craft and agile war canoes to those that could hold fifty paddlers or hunt for whales at sea, they have been described as 'the finest craft people have ever created'.[35] Broad and flat-bottomed enough to be paddled along shallow streams, and sturdy enough to be able to shoot treacherous rapids, they were also light enough to be picked up and carried around an obstacle or between two bodies of water; in the case of smaller canoes by one person, strapped to the back.

With its network of lakes and rivers, for many of the native peoples of the northeastern USA and what is now Canada (25 per cent of which is covered by water), and across the continent to Alaska, the birch bark canoe was the supreme form of transport, enabling long-distance travel for subsistence purposes and trading, and to access the territory of enemy tribes. But the use of canoes wasn't limited to the regions in which birches of the right kind and size grew. From prehistoric times, native groups traded both bark and finished canoes with others both to the north and south of the trees' range, and some were acquired via raids.[36] It was the skill of native canoe makers of the northeast woodland region and eastern Canada such as the Abenaki and the Wyandot or Wendat (also known as the Huron by the French), considered to have been the most advanced trading nation at the time and who were renowned for making canoes of great size and strength, that was to enable European traders and explorers, from the 1500s onwards, to develop the lucrative trade in beaver skins. The brutal 'Beaver Wars' that took place during the middle of the seventeenth century throughout the St Lawrence and lower Great Lakes region had a huge impact, as colonial powers allied themselves with native peoples (the Dutch and then the English with the Mohawks and other nations of the Iroquois Confederacy, and the French with the Algonquian-speaking Wendat), and exploited local rivalries to gain territorial supremacy and control of the fur trade. As well as the slaughter of people and animals on an enormous scale, and the displacement of native peoples, the fur trade created great demand for birch bark canoes that were much bigger than those normally made. Estimates of their size vary – some say up to 11.5 m (38 ft) in length,[37] purpose-built to carry heavy cargoes of furs, travelling over huge distances for months at a time. After the French set up the first known canoe factory in Quebec, in about 1750 enormous

Shoes made by George Cleverley & Co. Ltd., from Russia leather dating from 1786.

stockpiles of bark were kept at canoe yards, such as that operated at Fort William.[38]

To make a canoe, a tall, mature birch with thick, hole-free bark and as few branches as possible would be selected. Of the various regional species well known to Native Americans (including the yellow birch, the sweet birch and the river birch) it was the paper or white birch (which has, unsurprisingly, also come to be known as the canoe birch) that was particularly favoured. Distributed right across North America from the Atlantic to the Pacific coasts and growing into large, stately trees with a single trunk, canoe birches can reach heights of up to 30 m (98 ft). It was the particular properties of the inner bark of these grand trees, now scarce in many former tribal lands, which had great thickness, strength and flexibility, that made them so suitable for making canoes. Such bark only develops in the colder areas of the north – the warmer the temperature, the thinner the bark – which is much less useful for waterproofing. Once a suitable tree was found and felled, a length of bark, determined by the size of boat required, was removed by splitting down the tree's length and then carefully prising it off. With the inside facing downwards, the bark was spread on even ground to prevent twisting, and carefully flattened beneath a template of the desired shape. The edges were then bent upwards and, held in position with stakes placed in the ground at intervals which marked out the curved form of the sides, bent further to take the shape of the canoe.

Because of its lightness, ease of splitting, durability and strength, northern white cedar (*Thuja occidentalis*) was the wood of choice for the sturdy laminated sections that formed the bow and stern, as well as the ribs that, bent to shape, formed the interior skeleton of the canoe and which were positioned along its length at intervals in a laborious process. The gunnels, which ran along the top of each side and which held the birch bark edge, were again typically made from long shaped pieces of cedar wood. They, along with additional pieces of bark needed to raise the height of the side of the boat in the middle, were sewn into position with black spruce (*Picea mariana*) roots, where available, which had been split and soaked to make them supple, though animal hide was also used. Cordage used to secure interior sections was often made of inner basswood (*Tilia americana*) or inner cedar bark. Inside the canoe, fine strips of cedar or birch bark formed a lining and large sheets were sometimes sewn together to make kneeling pads or cushions. To make the whole thing watertight, the holes made for the stitching and any cracks that may have appeared could be sealed with birch tar, or with pine or spruce resin that was traditionally heated with bear or other animal fat and powdered charcoal to make it less brittle. The outside was often decorated by etching or painting the bark.[39] The resulting canoe was highly manoeuvrable, but travelling at speed along fast-flowing rivers or through turbulent water where rocks or branches lay submerged meant that damage was sometimes sustained. If bark of the right thickness and flexibility had been used, however, it was generally not this that was damaged, but the wooden ribs, though these could easily be repaired. Spare rolls of bark, which could be stored for later use for several years, as well as cordage and sealant pitch were often carried on voyages. When not in use the canoe itself was generally stored away from light and moisture or submerged under water using rocks as weights.

A Cree-style 'crooked' birch bark canoe built in 2011 by Ferdy Goode.

The prow of a birch bark canoe constructed in the Algonquin tradition, being stitched with split sprice roots.

Another iconic symbol of Native American life quite literally shaped by birch bark was the wigwam. The English word is said to be derived from the term for a birch bark house or shelter used by the Abenaki, *wigwôm*, itself very similar to terms used by a number of other Algonquian-speaking peoples (prefixed by *wigwa* or *wikia*, indicating birch bark). The Abenaki are just one of the numerous members of the northeast woodland cultural group of the Great Lakes region, including the Ojibwe, Fox, Mohegan, Mohican, Potawatomi and Wendat, who used wigwams and whose tribal homelands extended across what is now New England and southeastern Canada, west to Minnesota and south to the Ohio River. Unlike the tepee, associated with the nomadic peoples of the Great Plains, and which was conical in shape, the wigwam, made from a framework of supple branches or poles, sometimes of yellow birch, and strengthened with hoops around the circumference, was generally dome-shaped. Sheets of birch bark stitched together with basswood or cedar cordage were tied to this framework working from the bottom up, to form the walls and roof. Other materials such as mats of woven *tule* sedge, blankets and hides, held in place by ropes and poles, might also be added. A semi-permanent structure, it could be partially dismantled, the bark and other coverings rolled up for future use, while the wooden frame was left in place. This allowed people to live in the same location for months at a time, tending their crops, then, as needed, for example during the hunting season or when fish were spawning, to move to a new location, often splitting off into smaller groups. Varying in size, but commonly some 3–5 m (10–16 ft) across, wigwams contained a central hearth around a fire-pit and sleeping platforms, making them warm and comfortable.

During the winter, however, and because of inter-tribal war-fare, the Abenaki and some other Algonquian tribes, including the Mohican, as well as Iroquoian peoples such as the Mohawk, lived in large, oval long-houses, some of them 60 m (200 ft) long and able to house twenty families, which also used birch bark for walls and roof-ing. Some groups of these often double-walled, well-insulated long-houses came to form permanent settlements, many defended by palisades. It is recorded that sheets of birch bark were traded to European colonists for use in the construction or waterproofing of their own houses. In 1680 'two sheets of bark', for example, were exchanged for a shirt at a trading post on the Straits of Mackinac in the Great Lakes region.[40] The use of bark as construction material was widespread across northern North America: from Newfoundland furthest east, home of the Beothuk, whose lavish use of red ochre may have made them the original 'Red Indians',[41] to the semi-subterranean wooden-framed winter houses constructed by Athabaskan peoples in Alaska, in which moss and sods of earth insulated and held bark roofs in place. Used too in northern Pakistan as a roof covering, in Scandi-navia its strength and flexibility, and the all-important waterproof

George Harlow White, 'A birch bark Wigwam and Chippewa Indians, Rama Indian Reserve (Ontario)', 1876, pencil illustration. Wigwams were usually dome-shaped.

and decay-resistant properties of bark, made it the ideal material for use as an efficient water- and damp-proof course (a use to which it is said to have been put to line the vaults of the Kremlin)[42] in traditional turf or sod houses.

Roofs formed from birch bark and turf were the kind most commonly used on rural log buildings across large parts of Scandinavia until the late nineteenth century. Although bitumen roofing felt is more likely to replace it in turf roof construction today, this component of the original 'green roof' is being used once more in some Scandinavian homes. Working from the eaves upwards sheets of outer bark are laid, inner side uppermost, directly on top of the roof boards so that they overlap like shingles, straddling the roof's ridge and also projecting along the eaves. While between two and six were traditionally considered sufficient, roofs of high quality might be covered with up to sixteen layers of bark. Expected to last for some thirty years or more, the bark is held in position simply by the weight of two layers of turf, ideally cut from good-quality pastureland in sections. While the first is placed grass-side down, the second layer has the grass facing upwards, the roots of this layer eventually growing down into the one beneath to make one firm structure, and in time ideally forming a flower-filled meadow.

In Finland farm buildings constructed from logs were traditionally roofed in a similar way but the birch bark sheets were overlain
with timber poles, interlocking at the roof ridge and tied in place
with tree-root bindings at the gable ends. Rocks might also be placed
on the roof to add further weight. As with turf houses, this tradition
has been revived in recent years, especially for the restoration of old
buildings now used as open-air museums. Like Siberian peoples such
as the Evenki and Khanty who relied on it along with reindeer skins
to cover the conical-shaped tents of their winter camps, the Sami of
Scandinavia had a detailed understanding of the capacities of bark,
applying it as overlapping sheets to the poles of some traditional
goahti houses before covering these with turf. A resurgence of interest

An illustration by John White, drawn in 1585, of the Algonquian settlement of
Pomeiock in Virginia, USA, showing buildings covered with birch bark.

in birch bark, which can be bought by the square foot, by modern designers in North America and Europe has seen this highly versatile material being used for all manner of decorative furnishing purposes, from panelling for cupboards, walls and ceilings to household objects, from candle holders and lampshades to egg cups.

Beyond our most basic material needs, for thousands of years birch bark has provided a pre-eminent material on which to record and spread our thoughts and beliefs: paper. Thin bark sheets form some of the oldest writing paper in existence. Exceptionally durable and water-resistant, it has been used by many cultures round the world. Since ancient times the people of the Kashmir region have relied on the thin, shiny outer bark of the Himalayan birch, or *bhurja* in Sanskrit (also translatable as 'leaf made of birch bark for writing on'), for the recording of texts and scriptures.[43] These include what are thought to be the oldest surviving manuscripts written in any Indo-European language and the earliest known versions of important Buddhist texts.

Waterproofing layers of birch bark beneath the turf roof of a log building in Oslo, Norway.

Probably produced in eastern Afghanistan in the first half of the first century CE, these texts comprise fragments of bark some 12–22 cm (5–9 in.) in width, glued and sewn together to form scrolls, the longest being some 2.1 m (7 ft) long. They are believed to have originally been part of a much larger set of texts and to have already been in a very fragile state when they were stored in clay jars some two thousand years ago. Written on both sides of the bark, the texts include various commentaries and *sutras* and a *Dhammapada* – a collection of sayings in verse form ascribed to Buddha. The Kashmir region became an important centre of Hinduism and later Buddhism in the first half of the first millennium CE, and it seems reasonable to conclude that birch bark paper (referred to in Sanskrit as *bhurja patra* or *bhoj patra*), which was also exported from Kashmir to other parts of India and central Asia, played a significant role in the spread of these beliefs.[44] Several collections of early birch bark documents written in Sanskrit (including the Gilgit manuscripts) now exist. Discovered in northern India, Pakistan, Afghanistan, Nepal and western China, they deal with a range of subjects including maths, philosophy and medicine.

Gracing the foothills of the Himalayas, thought to be the home of the Hindu gods, *B. utilis* has long been regarded in this region as a sacred tree, able to drive away bad spirits.[45] Its bark is still in use in parts of India and Nepal for the writing of sacred *mantras*, and for *yantras* (mystical diagrams used by Hindus to communicate with deities, and to ask for protection from trouble of different kinds), sometimes worn as an amulet around the neck or wrist. Some claim that only a *yantra* written on birch bark, which is said to have been 'energized', can overcome troubles and problems. Lord Shiva's attendants were said to have worn clothing of birch bark.[46] Other uses have included the wrapping of butter, umbrella coverings, roofing material, various medicines and the lining of hookah tubes. The enormous natural range of *B. utilis*, stretching from Afghanistan to western China, means that four regional sub-species are now recognized by experts.[47] Sadly, the sacred status of these trees hasn't prevented their serious decline

Fragments of a Buddhist birch bark text produced in Ghandara, an ancient kingdom
in northern Pakistan and eastern Afghanistan, in the first century CE.

in some parts of Kashmir, caused by illegal cutting for firewood and, ironically, through damage sustained during religious pilgrimages to the region. Serious efforts have been made to re-establish birch communities however.

On the other side of the Himalayas, far to the north, the bark of silver and downy birches was also being used to write on. At numerous locations in Russia, mostly west of Moscow and in Ukraine and Belarus, but most importantly at Novgorod, one of Russia's most ancient and historically important cities, discoveries of over a thousand bark documents indicate that this was a common form of communication here (and in northern and eastern Europe) long ago. Surrounded by birch forests, Novgorod, which had by the mid-ninth century become the political centre of the enormous territory inhabited by Slavic and Finno-Ugric peoples (stretching from the Baltic region in the west to the Urals in the east), stands on what was a major medieval trade route connecting Scandinavia with the Eastern Roman Empire or Byzantium. At its height during the fourteenth century it had become one of the largest cities in Europe and an important centre of art, literacy and Christian orthodoxy. The first bark document, retrieved in 1951 in a remarkable state of preservation because of the water-logged clay soil that had surrounded it for six centuries, was given a date of approximately 1400; the whole collection spans roughly the twelfth to fifteenth centuries.[48]

Written without the use of ink, by scratching onto the soft thin layers of outer bark with a bone, bronze or iron stylus, the documents, or *beresti*, are mostly ordinary letters written in a local dialect about personal or business matters, but they indicate an impressive level of literacy and have altered what had been presumed about the language and culture of medieval eastern Slavic people. One, produced in the early thirteenth century, is the earliest existing document in any Finnic language. Of particular interest is the collection of some seventeen items, comprising notes and drawings made by a young boy, Onfim, in about 1260. Much of the writing, which consists of homework exercises, is citation from the Book of Psalms, but it also includes alphabet and syllable practice, while the drawings include a picture of Onfim himself as a fantastical animal, as well as horses, arrows and knights.[49]

It wasn't only in ancient Russia that birch bark was used extensively as notepaper. With no other material available, victims of Soviet repression sent to prisons and forced settlements, and in

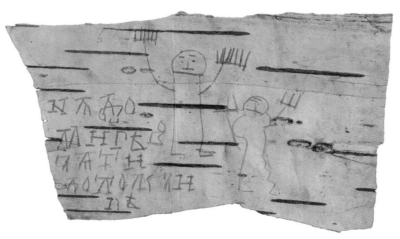

Spelling lessons and drawings scratched onto birch bark by Onfim, a young boy who lived in Novgorod in the 13th century.

particular Gulag labour camps in Siberia, used birch bark strips to write letters to their families. Nineteen letters written on birch bark between 1941 and 1956 by just nine of the 167,000 Latvians and Lithuanians, including thousands of children, who were sent to Siberia, have survived and are now held in a number of Latvian museums. A further 24 letters, written between 1943 and 1965, have also been archived.[50] As testament to the human rights violations and associated horrors of the Soviet era, these letters have been included in the UNESCO 'Memory of the World' programme.[51] In Transylvania pieces of silver birch bark were also used as postcard substitutes during the First World War.

Across the Atlantic, many thousands of miles away, the bark of another species, the aptly named paper birch, was being used by Native Americans of the northern forests for 'cartography, winter counts, medical formulas and tribal history' and what were described as 'old birch bark mnemonic songs'.[52] Inscribed with a stylus made of bone, metal or wood, charcoal or red ochre was rubbed into the marks to give them prominence. They were often interpreted dismissively as 'hieroglyphs' or 'coats of arms' by Europeans from the seventeenth to nineteenth centuries. In 1624 the missionary Gabriel Sagard observed:

> Each town or village of the Hurons had its special coat of arms which the travellers erected along the route when they wished it known that they had passed there. In one case . . . the coat of arms . . . was painted on a piece of birch bark as large as a sheet of paper. It consisted of a roughly outlined canoe, drawn in it were as many black strokes as there were men on the trip.

Weighted with a piece of wood at the bottom, this sign was then 'hung on the top of a pole stuck in the ground so that it leaned over a little'.[53] In 1779 it was noted, of the Native Americans in the Delaware region:

Some markings point out places where a company of Indians have been hunting, showing the number of nights they spent there, the number of deer, bears and other game killed during the hunt. The warriors sometimes paint their own deeds and adventures . . . Of writing they know nothing except the painting of hieroglyphics . . . which they very well know how to interpret. These drawings in red . . . may be legible for fifty years. After a hero has died, his deeds may therefore be kept in mind for many years by these markings.[54]

Scrolls, such as the *wiigwaasabak* used by the Ojibwe, which could be up to several metres long, were made by sewing several pieces of bark together using *watap*. They were used to record complex stories, ancient teachings and information for ceremonial or healing use, which could be memorized, with the help of pictures, and passed on. Tribal elders recopied them from time to time and they were kept in cylindrical birch bark boxes, often stored underground or in caves.

Prominent among these are those of the *Midewiwin*, the major religious society, or institution, of Ojibwe healers that trained men and women in the practice of spiritual medicine. Its sacred teachings involving ceremonies, rituals and magical song were recorded on birch bark scrolls invested with great power, bearing inscriptions and pictographic representations.

Europeans, including Thomas Jefferson, who had discovered that it was 'less liable to injury from damp than common paper', found bark paper extremely useful for their own purposes.[55] It was reported by naturalist Philip Henry Gosse in 1840 that

The outer bark of the birch is composed of many very thin layers, which may by patience be separated, and can be written on as easily as paper. The outer laminae are of a delicate cream colour, but as they approach the inner bark they become redder.[56]

A letter written on birch bark by Rasma Kraukle, a Latvian prisoner in Siberia,
on 19 May 1945.

Another visitor, a soldier in the French army who described himself as Monsieur le Baron de Lahontan, had already noted over a hundred years earlier that he had 'frequently made use of 'em for want of Paper, in writing the Journal of my Voyages'.[57]

Some of the oldest maps of North America were created on birch bark by Native Americans for use by explorers and traders. Tragically, such cooperation could only have hastened the genocidal demise of the people and their traditional way of life.

Beneath its bark layers, birch wood – almost as versatile – offers an equally impressive array of uses. Excavations at the site of Vindolanda, one of the Romans' smallest but most heavily defended forts and what was to become a major construction base for Hadrian's Wall, in Northumberland, have revealed what are currently Britain's oldest surviving handwritten documents, the Vindolanda tablets.[58] Written almost two thousand years ago on very fine slivers of birch, as well as alder and oak wood, they provide an unparalleled source of information about life in Roman Britain on its northern frontier. The tablets were voted 'Britain's top treasure' in 2003. Known to have been a fort by the late 80s CE, Vindolanda underwent several phases of construction before being demolished. A new structure was erected (which served as a garrison) when Hadrian's wall (designed to control the movements of local tribes and regulate trade between the Romans and their heathen neighbours) was begun in around 120 CE.

Dating from 92–103 CE and bearing writing in ink made from carbon, gum arabic and water – the earliest known examples of the use of ink lettering in Roman times – the tablets were preserved deep down in oxygen-free deposits, many in a waterlogged former rubbish dump near the commander's house. Since the ink was badly faded in most, infrared photography has helped make the writing more visible. Up to just 3 mm (0.1 in.) thick, and so fine they were thought when first discovered in 1973 to be wood shavings, these thin layers of wood were taken from local trees. About the size of a modern postcard (20 cm × 8 cm/7.9 in. × 3.1 in.), the sheets had been scored down the centre and then folded so that the text was on the

An invitation to a birthday party written on a thin sliver of wood in around 100 CE, discovered at Vindolanda in Northumberland.

inner faces and the address written on the back. Longer documents could be constructed by making a hole in one corner and tying several sheets together. These 'postcards from the past', most of which were written in Roman cursive script, allow us an extraordinary and fascinating glimpse into the lives of the ordinary people, military personnel and slaves living and working at the fort at the time. The topics recorded range from sets of instructions, work rotas, requests for leave and official reports about army matters to non-military activities associated with various trades and professions (from medical doctors to shoemakers and wagon repairers), requests for more beer and a birthday party invitation, sent in around 100 CE, from one Claudia Severa to her friend Sulpicia Lepidina. This last is thought to be the earliest writing by a woman ever discovered in Latin. One message written to an anonymous soldier stated that he had been sent socks, sandals and 'two pairs of underpants', confirmation, if one were needed, that Roman soldiers did indeed dress warmly in the inclement north.[59] Once the fighting between the Romans and the northern British tribes was over, in about 212 CE, the troops and their families left, and threw anything they couldn't carry with them into the site's defensive ditches. Among the remarkable recent finds at Vindolanda from this period are 421 shoes unearthed in 2016 – the largest collection of Roman footwear yet found within the Empire.[60]

While similar discoveries at other sites in Britain show that writing on birch and other wood was common in the northern provinces, thin strips were being used for other purposes elsewhere: in Siberia the Khanty still use paper-thin shavings of finely shredded birch wood for mopping up and wiping things clean and as an absorbent layer in cradles. Originally made from interwoven strips of papery bark, wafer-thin sheets or veneers of birch and pine wood were also once widely used for baskets across northern Europe. In Britain this industry was especially associated with the Tamar Valley on the borders of Devon and Cornwall, which had a long established reputation for flower and fruit growing. The making of these 'chip baskets' and punnets became a cottage industry there, so much so that by the late nineteenth century several factories had been set up in the region in order to supply the growers of soft fruit such as strawberries, as well as other produce including mushrooms, tomatoes and watercress, across the UK. Working with timber taken from local woods (and also imports from Scandinavia, Canada and Russia), young women standing at benches interwove strips cut from veneers to form the bottoms of the punnets, before folding them up to form the sides

Strawberry pickers from Calstock in the Tamar Valley, Cornwall, where a 'chip basket' factory was set up in the 1920s.

and attaching a rim with staples. A number of factors conspired to bring an end to this specialized industry in the 1960s: the introduction of compressed paper and then plastic, competition from imported fruit and the demise of the railways among them.[61]

With its fine texture and straight grain, birch timber is eminently suitable for veneers. Its particular qualities have led to some very specialized uses, none more so perhaps than in the form of plywood – sheets of veneer that have been glued together under pressure to form a laminate wood that is light, extremely strong and dimensionally stable. These particular properties have made it suitable for a great range of uses from the manufacture of skateboards and skis to the construction of aeroplanes. Perhaps the most famous aircraft to make use of birch plywood are the 7,781 de Havilland Mosquitos built in Britain for combat during the Second World War.

From the 1920s onwards, military aircraft in particular had begun to make more use of metal in their construction, but the Second World War saw a dramatic reversal of this trend because of the need to conserve scarce and valuable aluminium and other metals. Made almost entirely of wood, the Mosquito's streamlined shell was formed from low-density Ecuadorean balsa (*Ochroma lagopus*) sandwiched

One of the hugely versatile, high-performance DH98 Mosquito aeroplanes constructed from balsa wood and birch.

between load-bearing plywood skins made from Canadian birch veneers. This construction was extremely stable and needed no additional stiffening. The torsional strength of the plane's rear section was achieved by laying the birch plies diagonally so that their grains crossed at right angles round the frame. The wings also had outer skins of plywood. Even though the heat and damp of tropical environments were to cause problems with the wood glues, two important advantages of the Mosquito's construction were that it was much less easy to detect by radar than metal, and if damage was sustained, its panelled sections were easier to replace. 'The Timber Terror', as it was known, turned out to be a highly successful design.[62] Also conceived during the Second World War, the phenomenal H-4 Hercules was regarded by some as possibly 'the most prodigious aviation project of all time'.[63] Similarly constructed from plywood owing to the wartime restriction on aluminium and to save weight, it was colloquially and misleadingly referred to as the 'Spruce Goose' (a name its designer Howard Hughes always hated). It could have been more accurately entitled the 'Birch Bird'.

It was the largest flying boat ever built: some 66 m (218 ft) long, nearly 24 m (80 ft) high, with a wingspan of over 97 m (320 ft). Still the largest aircraft in terms of wingspan ever to fly, this enormous plane was made almost entirely of birch. Designed to carry some 750 troops or war cargo, such as two 30-ton Sherman tanks, across the Atlantic to Britain, as Allied ships were then suffering heavy losses in the English Channel, its construction was, in Hughes's words, 'a monumental undertaking'.[64] Decades ahead of its time, it was built by the Hughes Aircraft Company using a type of composite technology known as the 'Duramold' process, in which several very thin birch plies impregnated with phenolic resin are laminated together using pressure and heat. This method allowed the birch veneers (reputedly ironed flat by teams of girls and young women) and resin, together only some quarter of an inch thick, to be shaped to make not just the surface structure but the supporting frame as well. Although conceived in 1942, the Spruce Goose wasn't finished in time to be used during the war, making only one brief flight in November 1947. Its late completion and the huge amount of money it cost led to Hughes, said to have put some $18 million of his own money into the project, appearing before the Senate War Investigating Committee in 1947 for overuse of some $22 million of government funds.

Preceding the Mosquito and the Hercules, however, and using a process that has been seen as a forerunner of modern plastics, American pioneer aviator and inventor Harry N. Atwood from New Hampshire had built a monoplane in 1935, using a wood-laminating process he invented himself. At that time, during the Great Depression, when simple everyday necessities were hard for many to buy, he had seen himself as the 'Henry Ford of aviation'. Atwood was inspired by an audacious vision of creating a plane – the 'Airmobile' – that he said could be made from a single birch tree, so cheap and simple to make that there would be 'one in every garage': the 'Model T of the air'. 'Start ten workers making that airplane at 8 o'clock in the morning and it could be in the air by 5 o'clock in the afternoon of that same day,' he is reported to have said.[65] While an average plane of the time comprised 'thousands of parts', Atwood envisioned a 'one-piece' seamless craft. His advertisement ran: 'Not a wire. Not a brace. Not a spar. Not a piece of fabric. Not a beam. Not a turn-buckle. Not a supporting metal fitting. Not a rivet. Not a welding. Not a single joint seam or piecing.'[66]

Enlisting the help and expertise of a struggling furniture company (French & Heald) in New Hampshire, and drawing on his knowledge of chemicals and wood veneers, he invented 'Duply', a wood-plastic composite that was lightweight, fire-resistant and stronger than aluminium of the same thickness. The process involved layering extremely thin birch veneers with thermo-plastic sheets and subjecting them to heat and pressure. To construct the plane, birch strips about 5 cm (2 in.) wide and only hundredths of an inch thick were wound spirally over pre-made forms that were the size and shape of the main parts of the plane, interspersed with cellulose acetate sheets, until the desired thickness was reached. After clamping in

The Hughes H-4 Hercules, the largest flying boat ever built, nicknamed the 'Spruce Goose'.

place, the parts were insulated inside a 'rubber bag', placed in a pressure chamber and subjected to compressed air and then steam to soften the plastic. To solidify the composite cold water was dripped onto the bag. After the removal of the rubber and the forms, the hard-baked, shell-like veneer was ready to be assembled.[67] When Atwood's prototype Duply aircraft – a one-person, open-cockpit plane, 4.8 m (16 ft) long, with a wingspan of 6.7 m (22 ft) and weighing only some 362 kg (800 lbs) – was at last complete the Early Bird society of pioneer aviators announced that it been constructed from just 'a single birch tree, only 6 inches in diameter', repeating one of Atwood's promotional claims.[68]

An extraordinary character, part showman and confidence trickster who had at one time kept a bear, tame squirrels and a kinkajou as pets, Atwood's dishonest business dealings, mercurial behaviour and obsessive need for control meant that he bankrupted the furniture company and, deeply in debt, was obliged to sell his patent. The Duply moulded plywood process then became known as the 'Vidal' process and, with the shortage of aluminium, went on to be developed for use in numerous planes and boats that served (or were designed for service) during the Second World War before aluminium and other metals came back into use. A number of today's light aircraft, including gliders, that are home-built use birch plywood (in Europe mostly exported from Finland) in their construction.[69]

It's not just aircraft that have benefited from birch plywood, however. Harry Atwood had also experimented with furniture, canoes, prams, coffins, shoe heels, toilet seats and skis. An ancient form of transport used for thousands of years by peoples such as the Sami to help them traverse the frozen North (the oldest having been found in Russia, Sweden and Norway), many different types of ski, originally carved from solid wood, have been made for different purposes, different types of terrain and different kinds of snow during their long history. The availability and unique natural properties of birch – considerable strength and ability to bend and flex without breaking – made it particularly useful, however. Birch is still used as a wood core in some laminated recreational skis.

Perhaps Harry Atwood knew or anticipated that birch plywood would prove to be particularly important in the field of acoustics. It has a natural resonance that 'peaks in the high and low frequencies', which are also the most difficult for music speakers to reproduce.[70] The overall effect is to even the tone. For this reason, for many years birch wood was highly sought after for the making of speaker cabinets. The distinctive sound of BBC radio and TV broadcasts, the high technical quality of which came to be regarded as 'probably the single most influential body in shaping [the] public's awareness and expectations of high fidelity sound', was due in no small part to birch.[71] The requirement for the LS3/5A, a monitoring loudspeaker which played a key part in the production of this high-quality BBC sound from the mid-1970s, was that only birch plywood, which must be 12 mm (0.5 in.) thick, could be used for the construction of the main body of the speaker cabinet, every joint of which had to be braced with beech wood. Both the birch ply and beech wood were firmly specified, as BBC tests had found that other hard woods, such as Paraná pine, produced 'a clearly audible colouration due to interaction with a resonance of the bass driver chassis'.[72] Another repercussion of the special acoustic qualities of birch is its use for the shells of drums.

Producing a sound that is sometimes described as full and rounded or bright and punchy, with 'plenty of projection', birch-shelled drums are those most commonly available today.[73] Birch veneer is also used as a tone wood in some acoustic and semi-acoustic guitar bodies and for drum sticks.

Generally pale in colour, straight-grained, with no distinct heartwood, and often distinguished by a satin-like sheen, birch is much used as a furniture veneer. The unusual, rippled grain patterning referred to as 'masur', or 'Karelian birch' – terms used along with 'curly birch' to describe timber with a decorative grain in general – refers strictly speaking to that found in some silver and downy birch wood from the Karelia region. Its patterning has led to its use as a decorative veneer and for a variety of turned objects as well as architectural woodwork and furniture. Tough, strong (when well seasoned, resembling oak in hardness, strength and toughness), good for turning and generally lightweight, birch timber has been used in its whole form for countless purposes. Wigwam poles, spears, bows and arrows, toboggans, paddles, sledge runners and the frames for snow shoes are some of the uses made of it by the native peoples of North America and Siberia. The Mansi and Selkup of Siberia still make beautiful cradles from birch wood and bark. Across Eurasia, these and other items of furniture and household implements of every kind, from spoons and dishes to handles for brooms and tools, herring barrels, toys and footwear have all been made from the wood. While poorer people might have worn birch clogs in Britain, for the better off, it was the heels of shoes that were once commonly made of this timber.[74]

Since his seventeenth-century treatise was much influenced by the need to promote the restoration and cultivation of trees traditionally used in British shipbuilding, upon which the defence and trade of the nation at the time relied, it is perhaps not surprising that John Evelyn should have determined that 'Birch be of all other the worst of Timber,' presumably because it decays quickly when in contact with water unless made durable by treatment. He did concede, however, a long list of implements made from it, including 'the Husbandmans Ox-yoaks; also . . . Hoops, Paniers, Brooms, Wands, Bavin [a bundle of twigs used in broom-making] and Fuel'.[75] An unexpected use of birch wood, also recorded by Evelyn, was that of a cosmetic face powder for men. 'Lastly, of the whitest part of the old wood, found commonly in doating Birches,' he wrote, 'is made the grounds of our Gallants Sweet-powder.'[76] This use was further embellished by the inclusion of the description 'effeminate farined' in the last edition of *Sylva* (1825), a publication which also suggested that rotted wood made 'the best mould for the raising of divers seedlings of the rarest plants and flowers'.[77] Not long afterwards, among a large volume of other information, such as the use of Scottish birch wood for herring barrels, J. C. Loudon recorded,

> The Highlanders of Scotland make everything of it; they build their houses, make their beds and chairs, tables, dishes and spoons; construct their mills, make their carts, ploughs, harrows, gates and fences, and even [referring to the bark] manufacture rope of it.[78]

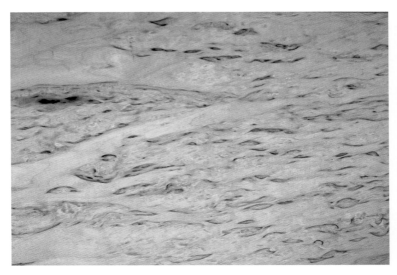

A piece of masur or Karelian birch, showing its distinctive rippled grain.

In Britain birches were widely managed and coppiced, so that they would regenerate 'in strong and lusty tufts' as Evelyn put it, from which selected shoots could grow to form the birch poles that were sought after by wood-turners. During the first half of the nineteenth century, as the Lancashire cotton industry was developing, English birch poles produced in this way were in great demand as the preferred wood for huge numbers of bobbins, spools and reels on which cotton manufacture depended. A significant woodland industry arose in the northwest of England in the Cumbrian region as small woodlands and thickets were coppiced to supply the mills. The manufacture of gunpowder from birch charcoal was formerly another important industry. Birch was also one of the commonest fuels for the ironworks of the Weald of southern England during the seventeenth century. Until the 1950s, it seems, a more curious use for birch poles in South Wales was as a chemical reagent in the copper industry. Freshly cut, they were thrust into the vats containing molten copper so that the gases these poles released on charring would remove the unwanted oxygen that had been absorbed by the copper during the refining process, which would otherwise lower the purity of the metal.[79]

Today, a range of items we use in and around our homes may be made from or incorporate birch wood, from flooring and work surfaces to the rungs of a rope ladder. Solid birch is also occasionally used for guitar bodies, and it's become the wood of choice for the handles of mallets used to play keyboard percussion instruments, such as the marimba, which must be rigid and strong yet light. Wood produced by the cherry or black birches, distributed across parts of eastern North America, takes on a deep mahogany colour with age, and was once widely used by cabinet makers as a substitute for this much more expensive tropical wood. It's still a significant timber tree, but the yellow birch – highly valued by colonial shipbuilders because of the rot resistance of its light but strong and resinous wood – is considered the most important of all birch species for timber and is currently widely used for furniture and cabinet making.

Most of the birch commercially grown worldwide today, however, ends up as pulp. It is one of the many woods that have found their way into commercial pulping mills for the production of paper and packaging on a massive scale. But its structure and characteristics have made it suitable for paper products of a particular kind, including greaseproof paper and glassine. Birch wood contains cellulose fibres that for a hardwood are relatively long and slender. They are also thin-walled and high in hemi-celluloses, which together mean that they intermesh well and make naturally strong papers. During the papermaking process, high-pressure rollers calender the sheets, encouraging all the fibres to flatten in the same direction, thereby increasing its smoothness, density and gloss. The result is a paper that is shiny, light and semi-translucent with high tensile strength. Often treated with various coatings, the grease-resistant and water-repellent properties of glassine have made it suitable for a number of applications where the protection of delicate materials is needed, for example, in books or albums as an interleaving paper (protecting illustrations or images from contact with facing pages) and for the separation or packaging of foods. Glassine is also used as a window material for envelopes and for the packaging of fireworks.

Finland, one of the world's largest producers of paper and paperboard, grows and imports large volumes of birch. Almost half of the approximately eleven million cubic metres of timber it imported in 2013 was birch 'pulp wood', mostly sourced from Russia and Baltic countries. The Finnish Forest Industries Federation reported in 2015, however, that the land area covered by birch (*B. pendula*) plantations had been decreasing in the twenty-first century because of seedling destruction by moose and a reduction in subsidies for reforestation, birch accounting for only 5 per cent of all seedlings being planted. It concluded that increased domestic supplies were desirable for the future.[80]

No part of the birch is without use; the thin and supple twigs (also known as 'spray') have proved extremely versatile, having been used for everything from 'whisks for frothing syllabubs'[81] to artists'

Cotton reels, bobbins and spools used in the British cotton industry were traditionally made from birch wood.

charcoal. For medieval house construction, they were perfect for roughening the surface of the daub (generally mud or clay mixed with straw or animal dung which coated the woven lattice of sticks or wattles) so that the waterproofing layer of lime plaster would adhere. In Scotland, Loudon recorded the common use of birch twigs for thatching, noting also that 'dried in the summer, with the leaves on' they provided 'an excellent material for sleeping upon' where heather was scarce.[82] This practice was employed too by the Sami who traditionally stuffed reindeer skins with birch spray to 'serve for seats during the day, and beds at night'.[83] Peoples such as the Nenets of Siberia still lash young birch branches together to form mats on which to place their reindeer skins. In Scotland birch spray was traditionally thought superior to any other wood for smoking foods such as hams and herrings, and across northern and eastern Europe and Russia in spring and summer it was an important source of fodder for domestic animals.[84] Especially in heathland areas, where other trees were scarce, it was important, too, for the construction of fences for livestock. A modern adaptation of this ancient custom is the continuing use of birch brushwood for steeplechase and show-jumping fences as well as shooting hides.[85]

In the Scottish Highlands, as in other parts of northern Europe, animal harnesses and ropes were once made by heating then twisting the finer birch branches. Baskets were woven too from birch twigs. They were important also as a fuel, notably in Scotland, for the distillation of whisky and in vinegar refineries, where bundles were placed in layers 1 m (3 ft) thick at the base of vats to help clarify the liquid. Another old use in Britain was revetting – the shoring up of embankments – and in Lancashire and Westmoreland (now Cumbria) the bottoming of roads crossing marshy ground.[86]

Perhaps the most famous traditional use of birch twigs in Britain is the making of brooms, or besoms, still carried out today by professional coppice workers, many allied to local or national associations that are helping to revive the traditional management and use of small deciduous woodlands. A variety of methods and materials, according to region, have been used to make besoms, a craft thought to go back many hundreds of years. The 'broom squires' who gathered their raw materials from the heathland areas of Sussex and Surrey and east Dorset were some of those who became particularly well known. The besom was much sought after for domestic use and the sweeping out of stables in the days before motor transport, and in British ironworks to brush away the slag that formed on the surface of the hot metal. By the late nineteenth century Verwood in Dorset had a large besom industry: 27 broom makers were listed in the 1841 census but it is thought that many more people may actually have been involved. Described in a 1926 report as 'independent, hardworking' people who lived 'in isolated places and [were] reserved by nature', entire families, including children of both sexes, were employed. John Haskell, one of the last two full-time broom squires listed in Verwood in 1939, started the profession at the age of ten.[87]

To make a broom, the handle was prepared first from birch or alder, or as often today a hazel pole, which was debarked and smoothed before being pointed at one end. The head was formed from a dense bundle of birch twigs (though heather was much used in the past) that had been cut in winter while the trees were dormant, then seasoned for several months (and sometimes boiled briefly to soften them) before compressing and binding together. Though the twigs can be pressed together by hand, various mechanical aids, such as large iron pincers worked by one foot, were sometimes used to make the bundles properly tight. Binding the twigs (done with steel wire today) was traditionally achieved by what were referred to in Verwood as sleets: thin shavings about 1 m (3 ft) long, skilfully cut from hazel or apple wood. In other regions lime bast, thin strands of ash wood, split oak stems, twisted hazel, strips of sweet chestnut wood, willow twigs or bramble fibres might be used. Once the bundle was firmly secured the handle was hammered into it with a wooden mallet, then a small wooden peg was driven in. Made in the traditional way, a besom can

Contemporary birch brooms, or besoms, still made to a design dating back hundreds, perhaps thousands of years.

Engraving of a Roman lictor carrying the *fasces*, said to have comprised birch or willow rods, as a symbol of authority.

last for many years. While some are bought today simply for ornament they are still widely used for domestic and garden purposes, on golf courses and croquet lawns. Light to handle and effective at extinguishing a blaze, birch brooms were considered up until the 1950s 'the best all round beaters for forest fires so far devised'.[88]

Sadly, it isn't just forest fires that were beaten with birch. The practice of 'birching' – beating adults and children with a bundle of birch twigs or sticks as a form of corporal punishment – appears to have a very long history. Birch trees have been so closely associated with this punishment for so long that some believed, as Loudon noted in the early nineteenth century, that the origin of the generic name '*Betula*' was 'from the Latin word *batuere*, to beat; from the *fasces* of the Roman lictors, which were always made of birch rods, being used to drive back the people'.[89]

It is indeed birch sticks or rods that are most often referred to as the component of the *fasces*, though other woods are also mentioned and it seems that willow was sometimes used for various punishments in ancient Rome. Associated particularly with the era of the Roman Republic (509–27 BCE) as Rome's control expanded over the Mediterranean world, the *fasces* were bundles of rods, sometimes including an axe (the blade of which is often depicted emerging), tied with a red leather strap, carried by the *lictors*, a magistrate's special officials and bodyguards. Having adopted it as a symbol from the Etruscan civilization, the Romans' stylized image of the *fasces* came to represent those who held magisterial authority. The bundle of rods, rather than one rod which can be broken easily, represented not just power and jurisdiction, but the notion of strength through unity. An enduring symbol, sometimes decorated with a laurel wreath, indicating victory, its use has continued into the modern world as a sign of the right to command or of collective power, adopted by various governments and authorities. Benito Mussolini's National Fascist Party chose the *fasces* as its symbol in 1919 and it is from this use that the term 'fascist' is derived.

As a widespread symbol in the West, however, at one stage depicted on the American dime coin, the association with the horrors of fascism has largely been forgotten. It is commonly found in heraldry, features on the Ecuadorian flag and can be seen in numerous locations, including the USA's House of Representatives, where large wall decorations embellish the side of the podium. The origin of the birch as a form of punishment appears to lie in the very ancient association of the tree with an innate supernatural ability to cleanse or purify and expel evil. Lunatics, it was believed, who were possessed with a malevolent spirit, were to be hit not as a punishment but to drive this bad spirit away. Wayward children were also to be treated and corrected in this manner, a practice alluded to by Shakespeare in *Measure For Measure*, as Duke Vicento declares:

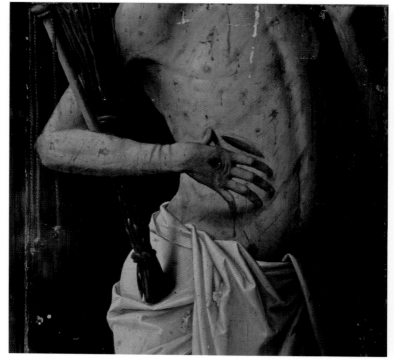

Circle of the Master of the Freising Visitation, *Christ as the Man of Sorrows* (fragment),
c. 1495.

Now, as fond fathers,
Having bound up the threatening twigs of birch . . .

Being hit with 'the birch' or simply 'the rod' as it came to be known,
however, could be an extremely painful and humiliating experience,
administered to men, women and children in all sorts of deeply
unpleasant and disturbing ways. Widely used for centuries across
Europe, in the colonies and in Britain's Commonwealth countries,
its practice was formally adopted by the Royal Navy in the 1860s for
boy seamen and in civilian courts at about the same time (for boys
and young men) instead of the cat o' nine tails or whip, becoming
the commonest form of punishment delivered by the judiciary and in
schools. While strong, smooth willow or hazel twigs were also used,

different kinds of 'birch' (in terms of length, weight and number of branches) were selected for the perpetrators of both petty crimes and more serious misdemeanours.

On mainland Britain during the twentieth century the birch was widely used for what was often referred to as a minor punishment for young men accused of stealing, aged up to fourteen in England and Wales and up to sixteen in Scotland. In order to deliver the beating the unfortunate recipient might be restrained on a 'birching table' – his arms tied together beneath him and legs held down with straps– a method last used in Fort William in 1948 on a fifteen-year-old boy, for shoplifting.[90] It was also ordered by judges for adult men convicted, for example, of robbery with violence. While birching was abolished as a judicial punishment on mainland Britain in 1948, its use continued as a penalty for violent breaches of discipline in prisons until 1962 and on the Channel Islands of Guernsey and Jersey it was still being carried out in 1968. On the Isle of Man (a Crown Dependency with its own parliament and laws), however, despite a case there in 1972 involving four boys which resulted in the declaration in 1978 by the European Court of Human Rights that birching was in breach of the Convention (and

'February – Cutting Weather – Squally', a steel etching by George Cruikshank published in *The Comic Almanack* in 1839.

A Latvian sauna whisk, made from twigs collected in early summer, when the leaves are at their most aromatic.

which the Manx authorities had tried to oppose), a further birching took place in 1976, and it was not until 1993 that birching laws were finally repealed.[91]

A much less alarming tradition continues in Scandinavia, Russia and the Baltic region where bundles of fragrant birch twigs are used as part of a sauna or *banya* to gently beat the body, thus activating the skin and opening the pores, while increasing blood circulation and relaxing the muscles. In order to soften the twigs the leaves are left on and sometimes immersed in water beforehand to encourage them to release their distinctive fresh aroma.

four
Sacred Birch:
Folklore and Tradition

A cross the northern hemisphere since ancient times, it seems, birches have inspired a special reverence and been regarded as holy or sacred trees by many of the peoples who have lived among them. As one of the first trees to burst into leaf, a signal that the world is waking from its winter sleep, the birch is a harbinger of spring, its delicate translucent foliage a symbol of new life and light returning to the land. In pre-industrial times, the pattern of the changing seasons was highly significant, indicating the right time to perform the various agricultural tasks upon which a community's survival depended. In Sweden, for example, as noted in the last edition of *Sylva* (published in 1825), the coming into leaf of birch trees was a sign that spring barley should be sown, and Linnaeus (1707–1778) was said to have 'exhorted his countrymen to observe . . . at what time each tree expands its buds and unfolds its leaves' as the best guide to agricultural activity that would ensure 'the foundation of the public welfare of the state and the private happiness of the people'.[1] The marking of seasonal change was highly significant in community life.

Associated with birth and fertility, the birch is widely referred to as 'female' in European folklore and is linked with ancient deities, such as the Anglo-Saxon goddess Oestre (from whom the word 'Easter' is derived), who represent spring. Another of these is the ancient Celtic fertility goddess Brigid (*Brigít* in Old Irish), also known as 'Bride', associated with the festival of *Imbolc*, one of

Imbolc Fire Festival held in Marsden, West Yorkshire, to herald the coming of spring.

four seasonal festivals, traditionally held halfway between the winter solstice and the spring equinox to mark the lengthening days and beginning of spring. Mentioned in some of the earliest Irish literature but later Christianized (by imparting the same name and attributes to a woman said to have existed in the sixth century and who was later made a patron saint of Ireland) to become 'Saint Brigid's Day', celebrated on 1 February, *Imbolc* was a time of feasting, and the lighting of fires and candles to represent a return of the sun. On 'Bride's Eve', in order to invite her symbolically to enter the house and to encourage her to confer blessings of health, abundance and protection on household, animals and crops, a figure made of straw, representing a child or '*dealbh bríde*', the form of Brigid herself, might be placed in a specially prepared cradle or bed.[2] A birch stick might also be placed next to her, to represent the 'wand' she used 'to breathe life into the mouth of the dead Winter'.[3]

Birch trees have been connected symbolically with the similarly ancient Celtic festival, known today by its Anglicized name Beltane. Held about halfway between the spring equinox and the summer solstice, and having survived as May Day, it marked the beginning of the second half of the year. At this time animals were driven to their summer pastures and special rituals, such as walking between huge bonfires fuelled with birch and other woods, were performed to protect, cleanse and ensure the fertility of livestock and people that had spent much of the dark winter indoors. The custom survived uninterrupted in Ireland and Scotland until the late nineteenth century but interest in the Beltane fires has recently been revived.[4] This was the time too when various trees or their branches were brought into villages and towns for decoration and positioned outside houses and in public places as a focus for spring festivities. In Britain hawthorn or may (*Crataegus monogyna*) was certainly one of these and has been described as 'the ancestor of the Maypole, the source of May Day garlands and the decoration of Jacks-in-the-Green and Green Georges'.[5] But across northern Europe, celebration of the arrival of spring involving birch trees was widespread and a birch was often chosen as a Maypole. We know that this was a practice in fourteenth-century Wales from the Welsh poet Gruffydd ap Dafydd, who wrote an elegy 'To a Birch-tree Cut Down, and Set Up in Llanidloes for a Maypole' lamenting that it had now been 'exiled from the wooded slope' where it had once been the 'majestic sceptre'.[6]

As a communal affair, celebrating the arrival of spring was a time of merry-making, however, and the birch tree would be brought to the village or town with much fanfare. In some places the tree or its branches were carried from house to house in the belief that merely to touch them would confer fertility and good luck. The birch, sometimes with its branches left in place, would be colourfully decorated with ribbons, garlands and flowers, and in Wales an effigy of a weathercock might be placed on top. Other trees might be used to make the maypole but commonly leafy birch branches would be attached. In southern Wales *Codí'r fedwen*, or 'raising the birch' as it was known, was a long-standing tradition after which the *dawns y fedwen*, or 'dance of the birch', was performed.[7] As an opportunity for fun and festivities, villagers would sometimes try to steal a pole, or in Ireland, a

Setting up a birch tree Maypole with the help of poles and ropes in Germany.

Maybush, from a neighbouring village, in order to benefit from its 'good luck', so some needed guarding all night. In Ireland the general revelry, often involving drinking and fighting, associated with these celebrations by groups of adults offended Victorian respectability and led largely to their curtailment there.[8]

Sir James George Frazer, who presented a detailed study of the traditions surrounding the celebration of spring and the arrival of summer across Europe in his epic work *The Golden Bough*, first published in two volumes in 1890, gave details of a variety of such customs involving birch trees at this time of year in Britain and across central and eastern Europe to Russia, versions of some of which are still practised. He quoted a disdainful account made by the puritanical writer Phillip Stubbes in his 'Anatomie of Abuses', published in London in 1583, which afforded, he said, 'a vivid glimpse of merry England in the olden time'. Stubbes had written:

Against May, Whitsonday, or other time, all the yung men and maides, olde men and wives, run gadding over night to the woods, groves, hils and mountains, where they spend all the night in plesant pastimes; and in the morning they return, bringing with them birch and branches of trees, to deck their assemblies withall.[9]

In Cheshire, on the evening before May Day, the 'May Birchers' would go from door to door 'leaving humorous messages' and it was customary for young men to fix a birch twig to the doors of their sweethearts.[10] Frazer noted the particular use of birches on dates adopted by the Christian calendar, including St George's Day (23 April) and Whitsun or Pentecost (a date from around the middle of May to the middle of June), that incorporated what would seem to be much older customs, and on 23 June, Midsummer's Eve, which had become 'St John's Eve'. He reported the custom of 'Green George' among the 'Slavs of Carinthia' (southern Austria) on St George's Day, for example, explaining that a young tree would be decorated with flowers and garlands on the eve of the festival and carried in a rowdy procession headed by 'Green George, a young fellow clad from head

Pieter Brueghel the Younger, *The Kermesse of Saint George with the Dance around the Maypole,* c. 1620–27.

to foot in green birch branches'. The costume, and sometimes the boy himself, if he hadn't managed to 'to step out of his leafy envelope and substitute the effigy so adroitly that no one shall perceive the change', was later thrown in a river or pond, a custom which, Frazer concluded, was carried out to bring the rain needed to make pastures green in summer.[11] He gave a detailed account of similar activities in Russia. On the Thursday before Whitsunday, he wrote, Russian villagers would go

> out into the woods, sing songs, weave garlands, and cut down a young birch-tree, which they dress up in woman's clothes, or adorn with many coloured shreds and ribbons. After that comes a feast, at the end of which they take the dressed-up birch tree, carry it home to their village with joyful dance and song, and set it up in one of the houses, where it remains as an honoured guest till Whitsunday. On the two intervening days they pay visits to the house where their 'guest' is; but on the third day, Whitsunday, they take her to a stream and fling her into its waters, throwing their garlands after her.[12]

'All over Russia', Frazer added,

> every village and every town is turned, a little before Whitsunday, into a sort of garden. Everywhere along the streets the young birch-trees stand in rows, every house and every room is adorned with boughs, even the engines upon the railway are for the time decked with green leaves.[13]

The activities Frazer was describing coincide with those of *Rusal'naia*, linked with the celebration of new vegetation and the old Slavic festival of *Semik*, held on the seventh Thursday after Easter. It was associated with *rusalki* – female water spirits who were believed to leave their domain in the spring to transfer life-giving water to fields and crops. In the nineteenth century, however, these spirits acquired an association with the souls of women who had met unhappy and premature deaths at the hands of men and were therefore believed to be intent on luring young men to their deaths. They were considered to be at their most dangerous at this time, having left the water to swing on the branches of birch and willow trees at night, and the annual festival was concerned with their expulsion, requiring offerings to be hung on the branches by peasant women to appease them.[14] *Semik* celebrations involving the decoration of buildings with birch trees and branches festooned with ribbons are still held in parts of Russia, where ceremonies dedicated to particular trees are carried out to transfer, symbolically, the fertile power of the birch to the land and traditional *khorovod* dances are performed.

Birch branches are commonly used as decoration by the Russian Orthodox Church today and carried by clergy during the celebration of Pentecost or Trinity Sunday as a symbol of fertility and the life-giving power of the Holy Spirit.

In some parts of Sweden on the eve of May Day, meanwhile, wrote Frazer,

> lads go about carrying each a bundle of fresh-gathered birch twigs, wholly or partially in leaf. With the village fiddler at their head, they make the round of the houses singing May songs; the burden of their songs is a prayer for fine weather, a plentiful harvest, and worldly and spiritual blessings. One of them carries a basket in which he collects gifts of eggs and the like. If they are well received they stick a leafy twig in the roof over the cottage door.[15]

The decorations or disguises used by 'Queens of the May', or 'May Kings', also made extensive use of birch. In Lithuania a pretty girl swathed in birch branches would stand beside a decorated May tree as part of the festivities, while in Germany the May King might be concealed inside a wooden frame covered in birch. Amidst much merry-making, his identity would have to be guessed, requiring forfeits of beer if incorrect. In Bavaria one of several young men disguised in tall hats of birch bark adorned with flowers would represent the May King, and be part of a ritual which involved making fun of local people, before his identity was revealed and he would ask for offerings of food. Concluding that the person disguised was regarded not so much as the image but as the actual representation of the 'spirit of vegetation', Frazer noted that spring or midsummer ceremonies – for which houses for both people and animals were

A woman from Suzdal in Vladimir Oblast, Russia, wears a birch garland as part of the *Troitsa* (Pentecost) celebrations.

A decorated birch tree being carried during *Semik* celebrations in Russia, to form a focus for festivities.

cleaned and decorated with garlands or 'crowns' of birch branches and flowers – were performed to confer this life-giving force. He stressed, however, the importance of the setting up and decorating of the Maypole and the festivities that accompanied this as part of a process of cleansing and renewal, the Maypole generally being burnt at the end. John Evelyn suggested that the birch's ability to produce large quantities of sap in spring could only be explained by its ability to 'manifestly draw to itself some occult and wonderful virtue'.[16] In some regions the tree and its sap were certainly attributed special powers of healing: in the Czech Republic for example, disabled people might go in secret to a birch tree on the first day of March ('the month of birches') and insert a piece of cloth with a drop of their blood on it into a cut made in the trunk. If the bark healed up and grew together, the malady was said to be healed.[17]

Some customs marking the arrival of spring or summer, including the tradition of dancing around a Maypole, have survived in the British Isles. In other parts of Europe, including Scandinavia, the ritual use of birch can still be widely observed. In Germany, notably in Lower Saxony, to celebrate Pentecost at *Pfingstbaumpflanzen* garlands and birch trees are positioned in front of houses and a decorated tree or garland stretching between two trees is erected in villages and towns. In Finland a tradition still exists of standing two silver birch trees outside household doorways to mark midsummer's day. Similar customs are in place in parts of Romania. Here, leafy birch branches are used to decorate the portals of houses, or positioned either side of the door, and on 1 May it has been customary for young men to place large branches in front of the homes of unmarried women (a custom also once common in Germany). They are used too to decorate churches during weddings, and for other special occasions such as confirmation ceremonies. The decoration of church pews with birch branches at Whitsun was widespread in England until the second half of the nineteenth century, and the tradition has been continued in the church of St John the Baptist in Frome, Somerset. Here, silver birch branches gathered locally from the Longleat Estate are fixed to the pillars that separate the nave from the aisles. This is done because the branches,

> being young growths . . . represent the renewal of life; and the stirring of the leaves resulting from the moving air currents in the church represent the sound of the 'rushing mighty wind' as the Holy Spirit descended on the Apostles.[18]

Such activities seem to also relate to the long-held and widespread belief in Europe in the symbolic power of birch trees not just to bring good fortune but to afford protection from harm of different kinds. One of these is lightning. On Whitsunday (and at Easter) leafy birch branches are still gathered in parts of Romania for blessing in church. In some areas these blessed branches are then burnt in the belief that this, along with prayers and 'a special magic formula', will bring protection from storms, an echo perhaps of beliefs such as those found in Scandinavian mythology in which the birch, seen as sacred to Thor, was associated with strength and protection from lightning.[19]

A birch-decorated garland is hung between two birches at the entrance to the town of Mechtersen, Germany, to celebrate *Pfingsten* (Pentecost).

As protective talismans, birch branches are also still placed on crucifixes in the Transylvanian region of Romania and at the sides of roads and bridges. In parts of the Balkans St George's Day has long been regarded as an auspicious day when evil spells can be broken. In the Albanian village of Novosej in the Kukës region, the St George's Day celebrations held in early May include the ceremonial collection, to the accompaniment of traditional music, dancing and singing by women and girls, of birch branches to be used as *potkas*.[20] A *potka* is a symbol of a powerful underworld force or spirit believed to have the ability to 'produce abundance and fertility and ward off alien and evil spirits'.[21] Families carry out their own private ceremonies, which include placing birch leaves in water with eggs, after which the water is used to wash children, and positioning birch sprays in places and among objects considered important in the home and garden, including vegetable plots and even the family car. The *potka* also has important symbolic significance as a traditional boundary marker, to ward off transgressors and protect against evil spirits, representing, it has been suggested, the following notion:

I am the ancestral demon of this community or family.
If you are not of my community of family, do not go [or]
allow your animals to go beyond the point where I stand
because I have the magical power to inflict evil and harm on
those who do not heed the sacred taboo. The community
will in turn impose a penalty or fine upon anyone who
offends me.[22]

While a mound of earth might also form the *potka*, a birch post or
tree was used in certain regions. Until the middle of the twentieth
century in Albania, the marking of village boundaries, performed
on the day of the spring festival, involved village elders in an age-old
ritual in which young people were ceremonially shown the traditional
boundary markers.

Performed elsewhere in Europe, including Britain, the ancient
custom of 'beating the bounds' (possibly derived from a Roman or
much older tradition of worshipping landmarks) was carried out
not only as a way of remarking and maintaining parish boundaries,

Patriarch Kirill of Moscow and All Russia, officiating at an all-night vigil
at the Holy Trinity Monastery of St Sergius, Sergiyev Posad, Russia.

Beating the bounds in Hungerford, Berkshire, in 1913.

but to cleanse and drive away the bad spirits or ghosts, which it was
believed resided around them and which could harm anyone who
interfered with them. During the procession led by church officials, parish members, including groups of boys, struck landmarks
along the route with (according to most accounts) willow or birch
branches. This ritual beating was also inflicted on the young boys
themselves at various intervals along the route – 'whipping ye boys
by way of remembrance',[23] as one Dorset vicar put it in 1747, or bump-
ing their heads on boundary stones, apparently for the same reason.
In England beating the bounds (which continues or has been revived
in places) is recorded as having traditionally taken place during the
week following the fifth Sunday after Easter, on what were known
as Rogation days (from the Latin *rogare*, to ask or beseech). Believed
to have been adopted in Britain in the seventh century and to possibly be derived from the custom of the Roman *Robigalia* procession,
during which a dog was sacrificed to appease the god responsible for
agricultural disease, Rogation ceremonies included fasting, prayers
and the blessing of crops. The Religious Tract Society noted in 1842
that 'until the Reformation', the beating of the bounds was 'observed

Boys and men known as *Gilles*, each carrying a bundle of birch twigs, during the Carnival of Binche, Belgium.

with much superstitious ceremony, often accompanied by drunkenness and debauchery in England' but that 'even after much of the pomp of these ceremonies was abolished, the processions and customs of ornamenting the houses [with "birchen boughs"] was retained'. Furthermore, 'a traveller' in 1657 had noticed as he rode through the village of Brickhill in Buckinghamshire at this time of year that 'every sign poste in the town' had been 'bedecked with green birch'.[24]

The ritual hitting or whipping with branches has survived as a custom in various parts of the world. In the town of Binche in Belgium, on Shrove Tuesday, during the highlight of the carnival that has been held there since the fourteenth century (recognized by UNESCO as a 'Masterpiece of the Oral and Intangible Heritage of Humanity'), up to a thousand men known as *Gilles*, wearing white masks and colourful costumes, dance around the town, each carrying a *ramon*, a bundle of birch twigs bound with willow, in order to chase the winter away and ward off evil spirits.[25]

Similarly, in the Czech Republic on Easter Monday (where, in the centre of Prague, a young birch tree is decorated with Easter eggs), a long-standing tradition is for men and boys to use woven and decorated willow branches (*pomlázka*) to symbolically whip the legs and bottoms of girls and women, in order to bestow good health and fertility for the rest of the year. (Those doing the whipping may be 'rewarded' with painted eggs or even a glass of *slivovice* damson brandy.) Such treatment, it seems, was commonly applied not just to women but to cattle or other farm animals in Europe. According to the folklore of the Scottish Highlands, a cow herded with a birch stick would become pregnant, while a pregnant cow, similarly treated, would give birth to a healthy calf.

For protection purposes birch twigs were considered particularly significant, especially with regard to evil spirits or creatures anciently associated with harm. In Romania, on the night of St George's day, some Hungarian Csángós still walk around the house three times, holding a birch broom – normally kept behind the door – in the belief that this will prevent 'reptiles' from getting into the house, though these beliefs are now said to be declining.[26] Birch twigs were commonly fixed above the doors of houses and barns to try and protect against, avert or undo the mischief that witches were believed to be able to cause people or their animals. Frazer noted that in parts of Germany on Walpurgis Night (also known as *Hexennacht*, or 'night of the witches'), on the eve of May Day, 'twigs of birch' were placed 'at the door and in the muck-heap to keep the witches

from the cows'.[27] A widespread belief seems to have arisen long ago that bad spirits could become entangled in birch spray and so could be trapped in this way. Birch brooms or besoms could therefore be used to cleanse a house that was thought to be bewitched. If a witch obtained some of these polluted brooms, she might use the twigs to make her own broom on which she could ride about the country to do her work. Women unfortunate enough to be accused of being witches in Europe during medieval times were depicted riding all manner of objects, but the association between them and birch brooms has persisted to the present day. In Scandinavia the Black Death was sometimes personified as an old woman or witch carrying either a rake or a birch broom with which she could wreak havoc.

There is then an essential ambivalence to the symbolism and associations of the birch (found also in its representation in litera-ture and art) with both darker forces and misfortune, and those that act as a power for good and which confer new life or protection. The concept of birch as a guardian tree is referred to in *In Lebor Ogaim*, a treatise in Old Irish (a language used between roughly 600 and 900 CE) on the Ogham alphabet and in the *Auraicept na n-Éces* (Scholars' Primer), thought to date from the seventh century. These sources explain that Ogma, an important figure in Irish mythology, created the alphabet for the learned and that the first message written in it consisted of 'seven b's in one switch of birch', which was sent to the Irish god Lug as a warning that his wife would be 'seven times carried away . . . into faeryland or into another country, unless birch guard her'. Written as ' ┬ ', and with the phonetic sound 'b', the first 'letter' of the Ogham alphabet was said to have been given the Old Irish name 'Beithe' meaning birch, since this was the wood on which Ogham was first inscribed.[28]

Believed to date from early medieval times, the alphabet was used between roughly the first and sixth centuries, possibly for secret or cryptic communication. Most inscriptions, found largely in Ireland

A birch tree decorated for Easter, Prague, Czech Republic.

and western Britain as a series of strokes and notches carved into the edges of ceremonial stones, consist of personal names and marks thought to indicate ownership. Comprising twenty characters or glyphs, only a few of which originally referred to trees, it is thought that a number were reinterpreted as epithets of trees in later medieval times, possibly as late as the fourteenth century. Incorrect interpretation of the composition of this alphabet by the author Robert Graves (who was influenced by various fictitious works and mistakenly determined that every glyph was named after a tree or shrub of which it was the initial) led him to propose erroneously in his novel *The White Goddess* (1946) that it encoded a set of ancient beliefs relating to the worship of a moon goddess and that it also presented a 'calendar of seasonal tree magic'. This was to set in motion '"tree zodiac" fabrications' and what for decades presented 'an almost insurmountable barrier to any serious study of the forms of astrology that were practised by pre-Christian Celtic society'.[29]

An illustration from *The History of Witches and Wizards* (1720).

Johannes Flintoe, *Old Birch Tree by the Sognefjord (Slindebirken)*, c. 1820.

The concept of a guardian or 'warden' tree planted beside a dwelling was once common in parts of Europe including Germany and Scandinavia. Such trees (including the famous *Slinde* birch of western Norway, blown down in 1874) were also planted on burial mounds. In a tradition thought to date back to the Viking era, and which still continues on family farms in parts of Scandinavia, a tree (the *tuntre* in Norway and the *vårdträd* in Sweden) was planted on the grave of the original farm's owner as a sign of respect towards him and his descendants, or in the yard at the centre of the farm to help assure its well-being. Caring for the tree showed respect to ancestors or the earth spirits believed to live in it and was such that the family whose house stood near it could adopt a surname related to it (a famous example being Carl von Linné (Linnaeus), who derived this name from the lime tree at his parents' home). In the past, damaging a warden tree was considered a serious offence. While longer-lived species such as ash or oak are generally more common, at higher elevations these guardian trees are likely to be birches.[30]

As offerings to the spirits of fish, pieces of cloth and money are hung from the branches
of a tree at a site sacred to the Mansi people, Siberia.

Slavic peoples too, traditionally believed that birch trees embodied special protective spirits; indeed, that at death people's souls 'transmigrated' into them. They were also thought to be able to ward off the 'evil eye' and so were planted around houses and in villages for this purpose.[31] During the *Semík* celebrations mentioned above, birches are still planted in a continuation of this tradition. In a version of the Cinderella story from Russian mythology entitled *The Wonderful Birch*, a birch tree assumes the role of fairy godmother. It grows up on the spot where the bones of the heroine's real mother, who has been turned into a sheep by a wicked witch, lie buried. Branches from this magical tree help the girl perform the impossible tasks that her stepmother sets her, even providing the clothes and the horse she needs to be able to meet and marry the prince of her dreams. In Russia, pieces of coloured cloth were traditionally attached to the branches of birch trees as an offering to the spirits, or a 'mother goddess' figure that the tree was believed to embody,[32] or to mark the tree's special significance to the spirit world, a practice that is still observed at sacred sites across Siberia, where over thirty distinct cultures are recognized.

To some of the indigenous peoples of Siberia such as the Buryat (the region's largest indigenous group, who live mostly in the Buryat Republic, in the vicinity of Lake Baikal) the birch, their most sacred tree, has been particularly important as a link or bridge between the earth and the realms inhabited by spirits. The concept of a world or guardian tree forming the central axis of the universe, stretching up to heaven or an upper world but also down to an underworld – a gateway facilitating journeys, in other states of consciousness, to other realms – is common to several world mythologies. At the end of the nineteenth century a study by two native Buryats recorded the initiation ceremonies a new shaman had to undergo:

> A characteristic feature of the first initiation was the use of a few dozen birch trees and one pine tree, which were freshly cut or pulled out with their roots intact. The trees were taken from the forest located near a communal cemetery. The whole procedure of procuring the trees was accompanied by sacrifices. One of the birch trees, which was dug out along with its roots, was brought into a yurt and placed inside the dwelling with the top of the tree coming out of the smoke hole. The tree symbolically opened for the would-be shaman an access to the celestial deities. This birch tree was usually kept in the yurt after the initiation ceremony was over . . . the rest of the trees were positioned in front of the yurt. During an initiation ceremony, each tree had a name and a specific function. People used trees either to hang shamanic accessories and decorations or to tie sacrificial animals. One of the birch trees was used by the would-be shaman, who climbed it and shamanized on the top, summoning deities and deceased shaman ancestors.[33]

Such ceremonies and belief in the sacred significance of the birch are still very much alive for many Buryat today. During the *shanar* initiation ceremony, a demanding ordeal undergone by an apprentice shaman to gain entry to the upper world in order to form a relationship with the helpful spirits residing there, a birch is climbed as a 'cosmic tree', believed to have nine branches, offering access to nine different realms or sublevels of the upper world. The souls of shamans are said to have been born and raised on this cosmic tree's branches, often in the form of eagles or other birds, before assuming their full powers. Once at the top of the tree, and as part of the 'ascent to the sky' ritual, the shaman may mark nine notches to represent the nine realms or 'shaman skies'.[34] During the annual ceremony referred to as 'Closing Heaven's Gates', held in the region's capitol Ulan-Ude to honour and thank spirit ancestors for the blessings they bestow, shamans call the thirteen master spirits of the Baikal Basin into birch trees brought to the ceremony, before these trees are ritually burned and the spirits they host return temporarily to the sky.[35]

Very similar beliefs were shared by the Yakut of the Sakha republic of northeastern Siberia. Each Yakut shaman was said to have been 'connected spiritually with a sacred birch',[36] on which his life depended, in the sense that he or she could use it to communicate with supernatural beings including spirit guides (to ask for help for example or to cure sickness). The Yakut believed that 'each clan or family had an animal protector which they were forbidden to kill or call by name', the spirit of which acted like the shaman's guardian and 'whose effigy on a copper badge was sewn onto the front of [his or her] costume'.[37] In the belief that 'the life force . . . inherent in the budding branch . . . could be transferred to other beings' among Samoyedic peoples, the soul of a dead bear might be helped on its journey to the spirit world by ritual whipping with birch twigs.[38]

It has been suggested that the spiritual significance of the birch among traditional peoples of the Siberian forests has been enhanced through its connection with the hallucinogenic fly agaric toadstool (*Amanita muscaria*) that often grows nearby. The fruiting body of this iconic fungus with its brilliant scarlet cap, flecked with white, contains the psychoactive alkaloids muscimol, ibotenic acid and muscazone, which if consumed react with neurotransmitter receptors

Buryat shamans calling master spirits of the Baikal Basin into birch trees.

in the central nervous system. Identified as the *soma* used as a sacred hallucinogenic drink from as long ago as 2000 BCE in India and Iran, these alkaloids have given it a long and fascinating history of use for religious and recreational purposes in northern Europe and Asia as a psychoactive and hallucinogenic substance.[39] In Siberia and parts of northern Europe, including Finland among traditional reindeer herders, fungi have been consumed in dried form (the ibotenic acid then converting to the much more potent muscimol) for religious and shamanic rituals. One effect of ingesting the mushrooms is a disturbed perception of space, giving the sensation of leaving the body and, it seems, the ability to communicate with other beings. Other people, as well as reindeer, were reported to drink the urine of shamans and in this way also experience psychotropic effects.[40]

Among some Siberian communities, talismans made from pieces of inner birch bark are also said to have been used by shamans for divinatory purposes relating to childbirth, and kept among a pregnant woman's sewing things to help ensure her child wouldn't be too big, making delivery easier. A dress made for the mother from these 'birch-charmed sewing materials' was to be worn during the

Fly agaric (*Amanita muscaria*) toadstools, fungi particularly associated with mature birch trees.

first week after the baby's birth. Later this dress would be left in a birch container in a remote part of the forest so that it would not be a source of 'contamination' to others.[41] Russian parents are also said to have once made similar talismans, *igrushki-oberegi*, as toys or amulets from inner birch bark in order to keep evil spirits away from their children.[42] This idea of the birch as a tree of spiritual aid and source of protection is found too among Native Americans. As the origin of so many of the essential raw materials on which their culture and way of life were based, providing shelter, warmth, medicine and much else, and providing food or habitat for animals such as moose, deer and beaver on which so many depended, the birch was viewed not as an inanimate object but as a living being, and a protective force in both the physical and spiritual sense. In the mythology of the Ojibwe and other Algonquian-speaking peoples who used this tree from cradle to grave, the first birch tree arose as the reincarnation of a young man, Wigwaas, who had died in battle, but who had been given the gift of constantly helping others in practical ways. According to the legend of Winabojo (a powerful spirit known by various other names, including Nanabozho and Nanabush) and the

Birch Tree, as long as the world existed, the birch would provide protection and be of benefit to all mankind. The tree received the useful properties of its bark and the ability to protect people from lightning as a reward for having sheltered Winabojo – regarded as 'the source and impersonation of the lives of all sentient things' and who also taught each living thing how to outwit its enemies – from attack by the mythical thunderbirds.[43] The story goes that, having tricked his way into the nest of the thunderbirds and stolen feathers for his arrows from their young, whom he killed in the process, Winabojo is pursued by the angry parents with lightning flashing from their eyes and their terrifying calls reverberating as thunder. Just in time, he takes shelter inside a hollow birch trunk but the

An illustration by Carl Gawboy for 'Nanabojo and the Thunderbirds', by Mark Sakry, published in *Lake Superior* magazine, 1992.

thunderbirds can't get him as the birch tree is 'their own child and he has fled to it for protection'.[44] Winabojo declares that from now on the tree will protect against lightning and that its bark will have many useful properties and not decay. But the tree must be honoured and its permission asked before its bark is cut. If people want to take the bark they must also place an offering at its foot and show their gratitude. The distinctive markings we see today on the birch's bark were made, according to some versions of the legend, by the lightning bolts hurled by the thunderbirds or by their sharp claws as they tried to grab Winabojo. Others say that they were made by Winabojo himself in memory of the event and that 'pictures' on the bark are images of the baby thunderbirds with outstretched wings. Another version relates that the marks were caused by the tree being spanked with pine needles and bird feathers for forgetting to protect an old medicine-man's camp from the trickster coyote, after which the tree never broke its promise to be of constant use to mankind.

five
The Lady of the Woods: Images of Birch

The sense that birches are mysterious, unknowable or 'other', and connected with the supernatural world of spirits and fairies – an image influenced no doubt by the appearance of their silvery trunks in moonlight – is one of the lingering perceptions that has shaped the trees' portrayal in literature and art. In Gaelic folklore the birch is associated with the realm of the dead, but also with a return from the grave. In old folk ballads, the birch 'wand', where it appears, has been traditionally used as a symbol that 'links the living with the dead'.[1] This association of birch is also suggested in the anonymous seventeenth-century ballad 'The Wife of Usher's Well', which was first published in 1802 by Sir Walter Scott (as one of the 'Romantic Ballads' in the second volume of his *Minstrelsy of the Scottish Border*), after he had heard it narrated by an elderly Scottish woman. The poignant song tells of an old woman (the term 'carline' implies that she could also have been regarded as a witch), whose three sons, who drowned at sea, return temporarily from the underworld in spirit form wearing hats made of birch bark, gathered from a tree that grows at the gates of Paradise:

> It fell about the Martinmas,
> When nights are lang and mirk,
> The carline wife's three sons came hame,
> And their hats were o' the birk.

153

It neither grew in skye nor ditch,
Nor yet in ony sheugh;
But at the gates o' Paradise
That birk grew fair enough.

Though the birch may facilitate the spirits' visit to their old home, they must soon return to their life beyond the grave. In his work on the myths, legends and folklore of trees in Ireland, and noting that birch has been used as a symbol not only of birth in this life, but as a symbol of life beyond it, Niall Mac Coitir has suggested that the 'resurrecting abilities of birch may also account for the cryptic reference in the *Cad Godeu* [a Medieval Welsh poem in which the legendary character *Gwydion* enchants forest trees so that they fight as his army] which states: "We have emanated from birches/ He who disenchants will restore us."'[2] A contrasting theme remarked on by Mac Coitir in ancient Celtic lore is that of the birch as a symbol of love. He gives the example of the fourteenth-century Welsh poet Dafydd ap Gwilym who 'asks a nun with whom he is in love: "Is it possible, the girl that I love, that you do not desire birch, the strong growth of summer?" Later he calls on her to come with him to the spreading birch.' Mac Coitir explains that the 'association of birch with love was a constant in Welsh poetry'.[3] In his *Complete Herbal*, Nicholas Culpepper, the famous seventeenth-century practitioner of 'astrological botany' (the belief that the position of the planets and other heavenly bodies influenced disease and the plants that could be used to treat it), described the birch as 'a tree of Venus', a designation also given to a considerable number of other plants.[4]

An association continuously referred to in poetry that mentions the birch throughout the centuries that follow is that of the tree as female or as a young woman, to which it is likened in particular via allusions to the slender shape of its trunk when young, and its drooping branches imagined as human hair. Thus, in his elegy 'To a Birch-tree Cut Down, and Set Up in Llanidloes for a Maypole', Gruffydd ap Dafydd laments that the birch tree, which he clearly regards as the poet's muse, is now

Henry Matthew Brock, illustration for 'The Wife of Usher's Well'
in *A Book of Old Ballads* (1934).

exiled from the wooded slope . . . with your green hair in
a wretched state . . . No more will the bracken hide your
urgent seedlings, where your sister stays; no more will there
be mysteries and secrets shared, and shade, under your dear
eaves; . . . you will not think now to inquire, fair poet tree,
after the birds of the glen.[5]

The tree has been defiled it seems by its removal from its natural
state. The comparison of the birch with a *finnbhean na coille*, or 'fair

Igor Emmanuilovich Grabar, *Under Birches*, 1904, oil on canvas. The painting exemplifies the association of birches in spring and summer with romance.

woman of the woods', was also commonly found in Irish Gaelic poetry and may have influenced the similar description, much quoted thereafter, coined by Samuel Taylor Coleridge (1772–1834) in his poem 'The Picture, or the Lover's Resolution' of the birch as 'lady of the woods'. Written in 1802, about 'a lover's resolution to forsake his love' and the impossibility of doing this, the poem mirrors the turmoil in his own life.[6] As the backdrop to his reflection upon the woman he loves, but who can never be his, nature, which is equated with a sense of freedom from the intractable problems and constraints which so beset humans, is expressed through the images of light and spring which the birch represents:

> I pass forth into light – I find myself
> Beneath a weeping birch (most beautiful
> Of forest trees, The Lady of the Woods)

Certainly the fresh beauty of its greenery in spring time and dappled summer shade, coupled with its graceful form, seemed to fascinate the Romantic poets of the eighteenth and nineteenth centuries, and so the birch became a symbol in their poetry of purity and beauty. At the centre of a movement that challenged the establishment of the day and the 'rationalism' of the era that preceded them, the Romantics believed in the healing powers of the imagination and were deeply inspired by nature. Used as a vehicle for the expression of heightened personal feelings and a child-like innocence of vision which they felt could help achieve spiritual regeneration (and a release from conventions and physical constraints), their verse was imbued with a sensual imagery and special reverence for the natural world.[7] We see this in John Keats's (1795–1821) 'silvery stems/ Of delicate birch trees', which he includes in his poem 'Calidore', a Romantic adventure inspired by Edmund Spenser's epic 'Faerie Queene'. Endowed with an 'exquisite sensitiveness to all the elements of beauty',[8] Keats was to be a major inspiration to the Pre-Raphaelite movement.

In Coleridge's later poem 'The Ballad of the Dark Ladie', published in 1834, the association of the birch with delicacy and feminine beauty is evident again as, with few words, he describes the scene:

> Beneath yon birch with silver bark
> And boughs so pendulous and fair
> The brook falls scatter'd down the rock
> And all is mossy there!

John MacWhirter, *The Lady of the Woods*, 1876.

William Wordsworth (1770–1850) too, as he likened the cascading branches of the weeping birch to the 'glistening tresses' of an imagined goddess, associated the birch with what was feminine, graceful and pure. In the 'The River Duddon', one of his series of sonnets published in 1820, the 'golden locks of birch' are used to help create the image of a 'personified figure of memory . . . a divine spirit seated in the heavens', but a figure who is, for all this, imprisoned in the 'stall' of time. Memory can be freed from the constraints of time however, because of the laws of association that govern it.[9]

> From her unworthy seat, the cloudy stall
> Of Time, breaks forth triumphant Memory;
> Her glistening tresses bound, yet light and free
> As golden locks of birch, that rise and fall
> On gales that breathe too gently to recall
> Aught of the fading year's inclemency!

Lord Alfred Tennyson (1809–1892), one of the most popular of the Victorian poets, also refers to the birch tree swinging 'her fragrant hair' in his allegorical poem 'Amphion' (1842). With the background of his own tragic experiences, however, he is noted for poems that deal with loss, sadness and melancholy, and it is Tennyson who is said to have first used the term 'silver birch' as a poetic epithet to describe the weeping birch, a name it has retained ever since.[10] It appears in the first verse of his poem from about 1830, 'The Dirge':

> Now is done thy long day's work;
> Fold thy palms across thy breast,
> Fold thine arms, turn to thy rest.
> Let them rave.
> Shadows of the silver birk
> Sweep the green that folds thy grave,
> Let them rave.

William Edwin Tindall (1863–1938), *Birch and Bracken, Adel Moor.*

In this poem about mourning, which emphasizes the peace that can only be found at death, and which goes on to state that nature's grief is greater than anything that can be expressed by people, the image of the silver birch links the reader with the notion of the other world, and also with the portrayal of sorrow, one of the themes with which the tree has been long associated in folk belief. In the *Kalevala*, the Finnish epic poem compiled by Elias Lönnrot (1802–1884) in the mid-1800s from traditional poems and ballads thought to date from the first centuries CE, verses of which were passed down by 'singing them to the tune of ancient melodies',[11] the hero Wainamoinen discovers the birch tree, which is 'enrobed in silver/ Silver-leaved and silver-tasselled', weeping because of the loss of leaves, bark and branches at the hands of people. It is only reconciled by a harp being made from 'sacred birch-wood,/ Fashioned in the days of summer,/ Beautiful the harp of magic', strung with the hair of a young woman.[12]

These sentiments of loss and 'weeping' (a term that has been used metaphorically in Russia for the exudation of sap[13]) are repeated in the folk ballad 'The Count of Keeldar' by Sir Walter Scott (*Minstrelsy of the Scottish Border*, 1803) in which the grave mound of Keeldar is a place 'Where weeps the birch of silver bark,/ With long dishevelled hair', and in Scott's highly influential narrative poem 'The Lady of the Lake' (1810) in which, at the end of the first Canto, 'The Chase', 'The birches wept in fragrant balm'. The 'tragic status of being human, caught between the cyclical natural world and our own narratives of being . . . which on earth can only become loss'[14] is a theme that had in the late eighteenth century preoccupied Robert Burns (1759–1796), who greatly influenced the English Romantic poets. Burns used sensitively drawn images of birches, as found, for example, in his nostalgic poem 'The Lea Rig' (1792), where 'Down by the burn . . . scented birks/ Wi' dew are hanging clear', to explore this theme.

The American poet Robert Frost (1874–1963) was also concerned with the transience of human life and with another reality existing beyond or in parallel with it. In his poem 'Birches', published in 1916, influenced by a similar poem 'Swinging on a Birch Tree' by Lucy Larcom (1824–1893), he is torn between the opposing poles of reality and imagination. He regrets that he can no longer find the peace of mind he did as a child by swinging on birches and also that children are now occupied by other pursuits. By climbing the tree Frost yearns to reach beyond his everyday life towards a higher plane of existence, and is perhaps contemplating his own death, but as the birch swinger, he will always return, anchored to the earth just as the tree is by its roots. An escape from the difficulties of everyday life can only be temporary.[15] Employing the long-established simile likening birch branches to women's hair, Frost describes those that have in the past been bowed by the weight of ice:

> trailing their leaves on the ground
> Like girls on hands and knees that throw their hair
> Before them over their heads to dry in the sun.

He goes on to reveal his longing:

> I'd like to go by climbing a birch tree
> And climb black branches up a snow-white trunk
> Toward heaven, till the tree could bear no more,
> But dipped its top and set me down again.
> That would be good both going and coming back.
> One could do worse than be a swinger of birches.

The birch has been used also, both in poetry and prose, as a powerful descriptor of place and as an evocative and often nostalgic symbol of belonging. This is certainly true of its more general role in Russian culture, in which it occupies a special position, not only as a poetic image of spring and of light, purity and beauty, but as a symbol of Russia itself, intrinsically connected with the concept of the 'motherland' and present in numerous traditional Russian folk tales, proverbs, poems and songs. One of the most popular of

Birches near Moscow, bowed by ice and snow.

traditional Russian dancing songs, of which there are numerous versions, some with differing titles, is 'The Little Birch Tree' (in Russian often *Beryozka* or *Berezka*). It begins:

> Vo polye beryozka stayala,
> Vo polye kudryavaya stayala,
> Lyuli, lyuli, stayala,
> Lyuli, lyuli, stayala.

> In the meadow stood a little birch tree,
> Waving in the breeze, the little birch tree,
> Lyuli, lyuli, there it stood,
> Lyuli, lyuli, there it stood.

In the song, the little birch tree is also a metaphor for a beautiful young girl. Traditionally, the beauty of a young, slim Russian woman has often been compared with that of the tree. After the correct observations, the girl in the song uses some of the birch's branches to make musical instruments: three little flutes and a balalaika with

Russian dance troupe the Berezka Ensemble performing a *khorovod* dance to the tune of the song 'The Little Birch Tree'.

which, according to one interpretation, to awaken the man she loves. Appearing in published form in 1790 in what was the first significant collection of Russian folk songs (compiled by Nicolay Lvov, 1753–1803), the hauntingly simple and poignant tune is now the well-known accompaniment to the circular *khorovod* dance performed by a Russian dance group (the Berezka Ensemble), who appear to glide effortlessly across the dance floor on floating steps.[16] The tune of *The Little Birch Tree* was included by Tchaikovsky in the final movement of his Symphony no. 4 in F minor, Op. 36 and formed part of the musical score written and arranged for the 2012 film *Anna Karenina* by Dario Marianelli.

The popular Russian lyric poet Sergei Yesenin (1895–1925), whose work was also inspired by Russian folklore, wrote about or included the birch tree in several of his poems, notably 'Green Hairstyle' (*Zelenaja Pričeska*) written in 1918, in which the poet addresses the tree as if it were a slender young woman, and 'The Birch Tree' (*Berezka*), written in 1913 and subsequently learnt by generations of children, expressing feelings of nostalgia and belonging. Moving back to the continent of North America, it is, however, this nostalgic treatment and the romanticization of his subject that has drawn criticism of *The Song of Hiawatha*, the famous epic poem by American poet Henry Wadsworth Longfellow (1807–1882), first published in 1855, in which the birch makes several appearances, including:

> Give me of your bark, O Birch-tree!
> Of your yellow bark, O Birch-tree!
> Growing by the rushing river,
> Tall and stately in the valley!
> I a light canoe will build me, . . .
> That shall float upon the river,
> Like a yellow leaf in Autumn,
> Like a yellow water-lilly!

Written (like the Finnish *Kalevala*) in trochaic tetrameters, the poem, which was immediately popular, drew its inspiration from Native American legends and real people (using the name of a sixteenth-century Iroquois chief for its hero) but, in taking considerable liberties in constructing the tale, projected the image of 'the noble savage' in the process. As critic R. H. Pearce has written,

> in Hiawatha . . . [Longfellow] was able, by matching legend with a sentimental view of a past far enough away in time to be safe and near enough in space to be appealing, fully to image the Indian as noble savage. For by the time Longfellow wrote Hiawatha, the Indian as a direct opponent of civilization was dead, yet was still heavy on American consciences . . . The tone of the legend and ballad . . . would color the noble savage so as to make him blend in with a dim and satisfying past about which readers could have dim and satisfying feelings.[17]

In the modern era, without the filter of a romantic lens, the birch tree has continued to help define a sense of place imbued with a particular intensity of feeling. This is evident in the work of novelist and poet Nan Shepherd (1893–1981) who, in her extraordinary 'celebratory prose-poem' *The Living Mountain*, painted a vivid picture of the landscape – the Cairngorm mountains – she loved and with which she felt a deep, almost existential bond. Written during the 1940s but not published until 1997, and drawing on her 'lifetime of mountain experiences', the book has been described by Robert MacFarlane (in his preface to the 2011 edition) as 'one of the two most remarkable twentieth-century British studies of landscape that I know'. Using 'precision as a form of lyricism, attention as devotion, exactitude as tribute',[18] Shepherd writes:

> Birch, the other tree that grows on the lower mountain slopes, needs rain to release its odour. It is a scent with body to it, fruity like old brandy, and on a wet warm day, one can be as good as drunk with it. Acting through the sensory nerves, it confuses the higher centres; one is excited, with no cause that the wit can define.
>
> Birch trees are least beautiful when fully clothed. Exquisite when the opening leaves just fleck them with

A 19th-century engraving of Hiawatha, in his birch bark canoe.

points of green flame, or the thinning leaves turn them to a golden lace, they are loveliest of all when naked. In a low sun, the spun silk floss of their twigs seems to be created out of light. Without transfiguration, they are seen to be purple – when the sap is rising, a purple so glowing that I have caught sight of a birch wood on a hillside and for one incredulous moment thought the heather was in bloom.

Compared with the branches of rowans, which 'look dead, almost ghastly as the winter light runs over them', Shepherd goes on to describe the 'drifts of these purple-glowing birches' with a painterly intensity.

In painting itself, the birch has received attention that reflects the notions, concerns and themes also expressed in folklore, prose and poetry throughout the centuries. The extraordinary *Silver Birch Trunk and Branch with Rose, Lizards, a Snake, Toadstools, Butterflies and a Snail*, by Otto Marseus van Schrieck (1619–1678), a painter of the Dutch 'Golden Age', is a vivid, almost three-dimensional representation (in oil on canvas) of the birch tree's association with the 'non-human' and with death. Against an intensely dark background, the birch's silver bark glints in a sinister and otherworldly light. It forms the stage for a curious biological diorama featuring lizards and snakes – animals that were regarded as 'unclean' at the time, the 'serpent' also representing evil – and poisonous toadstools, in dangerous and deadly opposition to the rose.

This symbolism was to be used too by the most influential group of (British) figurative Romantic artists during the Victorian era, the Pre-Raphaelites. In rejecting the social mores of the industrial age of the mid-nineteenth century they placed special emphasis on the emotion felt by the individual as a source of aesthetic experience. Preferring romantic subjects, they idealized the medieval and with great precision strove to depict scenes considered noble, copying details observed in nature with great realism. The work of John Everett Millais (1829–1896), one of the founders of the

Birches in early spring, Glen Nevis, below Ben Nevis, Scotland.

Pre-Raphaelite Brotherhood (begun in 1848) and who became the best-known exponent of its style, was to influence many of those who came later. In his large, arresting painting *The Knight Errant*, the trunk of a silver birch which dominates the centre of the work glints in the moonlight (echoing the powerful imagery of Van Schrieck) as, in an act of medieval chivalry, a knight in armour is about to free a woman who has been stripped and tied to it. When exhibited at the Royal Academy in 1870 the painting was accompanied by a text written by Millais explaining that 'The order of Knights errant was instituted to protect widows and orphans, and to succour maidens in distress.' Identified in nineteenth century literature, as we have already seen, with the female gender and sometimes referred to as 'Lady Birch', the silver birch was a highly appropriate choice of tree.[19]

Though only appearing in the background, the birch is present again, casting a similarly tragic shadow over the figures, in Millais's *The Bride of Lammermoor* (1878) and *St Stephen* (1895). This ominous presence is evident similarly in *Ophelia*, painted in 1852 by another member of the Pre-Raphaelite brotherhood, Arthur Hughes (1832–1915). Concerned with the transience of human love and beauty, his tragic figure sits in a dark, swampy woodland next to a stream, the pallor of her skin and her white clothing mirrored by the eerie silvery sheen of the birch tree's bark.

The association of birch trees with the female and with loneliness, loss or tragedy is reflected in the art of a number of British landscape painters of the nineteenth century, such as Henry Dawson (1811–1878) and William James Blacklock (1816–1858), by whom they are generally portrayed as lone trees or small groups of trees in desolate or isolated places with which they seem to have been physically and imaginatively linked. They often frame a view of water or

Otto Marseus van Schrieck (1619–78), *Silver Birch Trunk and Branch with Rose, Lizards, a Snake, Toadstools, Butterflies and a Snail.*

John Everett Millais, *The Knight Errant*, 1870, oil on canvas.

Arthur Hughes, *Ophelia*, 1852, oil on canvas.

flank a path, with a solitary figure depicted walking, sitting or tending animals, as can be seen in Blacklock's *On the Banks of Derwent Water; Silver Birch* (1843), which presents a woman tending cattle under trees by the lake. Blacklock, who painted many scenes in Cumbria and on the Scottish borders, was admired as a master of landscape and of light and for his naturalism of vision. His work is regarded as a bridge between that of the Romantic painters, with their focus on wild and sometimes mystical scenes, and the innovations, still to come, of the Impressionists.

With a penchant for trees, another British painter influenced by the Pre-Raphaelites and their detailed representation of the complexity and beauty of the natural world was the Scottish landscape artist John MacWhirter (1839–1911). His *Lady of the Woods* (1876) portrays in muted tones a single birch as the graceful central figure in an untamed autumnal scene. Fascinated by bleak, wild landscapes, after 1870 Millais himself also painted many Scottish scenes, mostly in autumn or early winter, which evoke feelings of melancholy and transience. One of these is the highly atmospheric *Winter Fuel* (1873) in which a girl sits near a cart laden with birch and oak timber looking into the distance. Portraying 'a mood of melancholy contemplation', the painting was praised by contemporary critics for its 'workmanship

William James Blacklock, *On the Banks of Derwentwater; Silver Birch*, 1843, oil on canvas.

and for lifting realism into a new realm by the masterly use of colour'.[20] Millais's *Glen Birnam* (1891) is similar in feeling, depicting a solitary older woman, also with a red head covering, walking along a snowy track flanked by birches and other trees.

The frequent use of birches to frame solitary scenes, often of ordinary women or men engaged in daily tasks, was employed too by the Norwegian symbolist painter and printmaker Edvard Munch (1863–1944), for example in his *Landscape with Woman Walking by a Lake* (1880), *Birch Trees with Man Carrying Twigs* (1882) and *Autumn in Vestre Aker* (1882), using techniques that have distinguished him

John Everett Millais, *Glen Birnam*, 1891, oil on canvas.

as an important forerunner of the German Expressionist movement. Adopting quite a different style but similarly concerned with the transience of human life, Van Gogh (1853 –1890) in his magnificent pencil, pen and ink, and watercolour *Pollard Birches* (1884) depicts several rows of trees, with a woman and man (herding sheep) walking away from the viewer on either side. In a letter to his brother Theo, describing aspects of the natural world he felt so compelled to capture, Van Gogh compared another row of pollarded trees to a 'procession of orphan men', explaining that 'in all of nature, in trees for instance, I see expression and a soul, as it were'.[21]

The birches depicted in the *Buchenwald 1* (*Beech Wood 1*) (1902) and *Birkenwald 1* (*Birch Wood 1*) (1903) paintings by Gustav Klimt (1862–1918), regarded as one of the greatest decorative painters of the twentieth century, create a different atmosphere entirely. In what appear to be autumnal scenes, with leaves coloured in the rich golden tones he favoured particularly during his 'Golden Phase', very small dabs of paint achieve a shimmering effect of light, against which the birch trunks, executed with great 'refinement of design and emphatic patterning' appear flattened to a single plane.[22] Thought to have been painted by Klimt by looking through a telescope, the trunks have been likened to the 'columns in a cathedral created by nature'[23] and are regarded as part of a long tradition in central Europe of allegorical paintings of the forest, influenced, perhaps, by the region's rich folkloric heritage.

Vincent van Gogh, *Pollard Birches*, 1884, pencil, pen and ink, and watercolour on paper.

Gustav Klimt, *Birkenwald 1*, 1903, oil on canvas.

In Canada meanwhile, from around 1910 a 'new generation of artists' influenced by Europe's Impressionists, who exhibited as *The Group of Seven* from 1920 to 1933, were determined to challenge the notion that 'Canada's own vast wilderness was deemed by the art establishment to be too raw and wild to provide a suitable subject for the fine artist.'[24] Their aim was 'to find a visual language with which to paint their native landscape – new, modern, vibrant and uniquely Canadian'. Unsurprisingly, perhaps, birches feature in many of the paintings they produced, for example *The Guide's Home* (1914), an impressive portrayal of dappled light through yellowing birch leaves by Arthur Lismer (1885–1969), and *Decorative Landscape Birches* (1915) by Tom Thomson (1877–1917) who, though not an official member of the group, was associated with it as an important inspiration. The bold blocks of colour and stylized, flattened linear shapes of the birches in this painting reflect Thomson's skill as a graphic designer and the experience he had gained working as a commercial artist for a Toronto design company that produced images used, among other things, for the promotion of tourism and the railways.[25]

Jack Merriott, *River Garry, Killiecrankie, c.* 1954, oil on canvas.

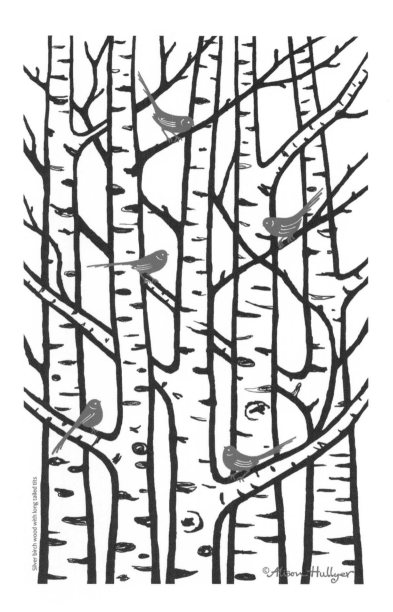

Silver birch wood with long tailed tits

Alison Hullyer, *Silver Birch Wood with Long-tailed Tits*, 2011, screen print.

Wu Guanzhong. *White Birches on Mount Chang Bai*, 1980s.

This decorative treatment is similar to the distinctive style adopted by British author, artist and poster designer Jack Merriott (1901–1968) to depict the silver birches in his striking oil on canvas *River Garry, Killiecrankie*. Merriott was famous for the artworks he created for British Railways and the Post Office, and this particular painting was used as a poster by British Railways (Scottish Region) from around 1954. The brilliant colours, especially the intense blues, deep green and red that contrast with the yellow of the birch leaves, create a clean, fresh look and a memorably vibrant image.

The silver birch continues to be a source of inspiration for modern artists today with stylized representations of the distinctive black and white patterning of its bark commonly appearing in a wide range of media and printed on everything from greetings cards and ceramics to textiles produced for a mass market. But individual images of birches, these iconic trees, continue to capture the imagination. In May 2017 Dukes Auctioneers in Dorchester, England, sold *White Birches on Mount Chang Bai (Zhangbai)*, a hanging scroll in ink and colour on paper, painted in the 1980s by Chinese artist Wu Guanzhong (1919–2010), for £500,000. Regarded by many as the greatest Chinese artist of the twentieth century, his works are said to 'bridge the gap between the past and the present and . . . perfectly articulate the fusion of Chinese and Western art'.[26] *White Birches on Mount Chang Bai* – similar to a previous work, *White Birch 1986*, exhibited at the British Museum in 1992 – demonstrates, according to Dukes, 'Wu's ability to combine adventurous technical and stylistic innovations with the time-honoured skills of the calligrapher's brush'. Wu Guanzhong described his work thus:

> The white birch is tall and slender, plain white, and on the trunk there are often marks which look like eyes. These eyes all give the impression of peeping quietly at people. They are like the eyes of a fair woman, whose tender gaze is reluctant to let you go. The white birch trees grow in the cold regions. I have painted several pictures of them,

and once wrote the lines: 'When the weather is cold, the ground is frozen and no flowers are in bloom, in front of Changbai Mountain (in Manchuria) I look at the white birch trees.'[27]

six

The Future of Birch

❦

These forests evolved under cold conditions, and we
do not know enough about the impacts of warming
on their resilience and buffering capacity.
ANATOLY SHVIDENKO (2015)[1]

The great ubiquity and popularity of birches, especially the
hybrids and cultivars of the white-barked species that grace
our gardens and cities, belies the serious threats that face
not just our rarer species in the wild, but those that populate or
fringe the vast, mostly coniferous forests of the northern hemisphere.
Studies are revealing that these boreal forests are seriously threatened
by climate change. Comprising just under a third of the total forest
area on earth, and containing an estimated 750 billion trees, they play
a hugely important role in regulating the earth's climate.[2] Together
with the peat-rich soil and permafrost they grow on, they also represent the single biggest terrestrial carbon store on earth, storing more
carbon than any other land ecosystem.[3] Rising global temperatures
are, however, a serious threat: boreal forests are proving to be one of
the world's ecosystems most severely affected, having experienced
annual warming at rates as high as 1.5 per cent in recent years, with,
it is feared, much worse to come.[4] The Intergovernmental Panel on
Climate Change (IPCC) has warned of potential future warming of
between 6 and 11°C (43 to 52°F) by 2100 across vast regions of the
north and studies show that as temperatures rise, climate zones in

boreal forests are 'moving northwards ten times faster than the trees' ability to migrate'.[5]

Fearful that a catastrophic tipping point may be reached in which forests change rapidly from absorbing CO_2 to becoming a major source of greenhouse gas emissions, researchers are calling for recognition of the crucially important role that boreal forests play and for increased attention at government and regional level to help address and mitigate climate change. Warmer and drier conditions have already contributed significantly, it is believed, to the spread of diseases and outbreaks of forest fires that have caused huge damage in Canada, Russia and Alaska. In 2014, fire destroyed some 3.4 million hectares of evergreen forest in Canada's Northwest Territories alone.[6]

A contributory factor to these fires is the spread of insects such as the mountain pine beetle (*Dendroctonus ponderosae*), whose life cycles have been accelerated by warmer temperatures, helping them survive the winter and to infest and kill large numbers of trees in zones that were formerly beyond reach. Native to North America,

The bronze birch borer beetle. Larvae create tunnels under the bark that disrupt the flow of water and nutrients to the tree.

the bronze birch borer beetle (*Agrilus anxius*) is a normal component of birch-dominated ecosystems, but can cause serious problems for birches, particularly amenity trees.[7] This beetle is one of the pathogens associated with the condition known as birch die-back, which typically affects trees that are already stressed by old age, injury or drought. Feeding on the foliage and then laying its eggs in the bark, the borer damages the tree by excavating irregular winding passages just beneath the bark on the main trunk, causing branches and the crown to die off. The tree may decline over a number of years or die in a single year if conditions are hot and dry. While *B. nigra* has been reported to be fully resistant to the birch borer and although other North American species in general have some resistance, European and Asian birches appear to be more susceptible.[8] The other main causes of die-back in birches are several fungi that may attack the trees when stressed or weakened by conditions such as drought. Although trees that have regenerated naturally seem to be much less affected than those that have been planted, birch die-back is just one symptom of a number of worrying environmental threats to trees in western Europe. The bronze birch borer beetle is not known to be present in the UK, but there is a risk of it being accidentally introduced.[9] Stephen Cavers of the Centre for Ecology and Hydrology in Scotland fears that much-loved and characteristic landscapes could be radically altered over the next century unless steps are taken to defend our trees.[10] He is concerned that:

> There is a clear increase in the number of novel pests and pathogens affecting the trees and forests of Britain. Most likely accelerated by the combined effects of . . . globalised trade, a changing climate and the planting of exotic species, the checklist of known threats has recently described an exponential growth pattern.[11]

Experts are calling for urgent action to be taken to stop not just birches, but other British forest trees, including oak, ash, Scots pine, larch, beech and juniper, from devastation by the new diseases caused by a 'host of new bugs, fungi and bacteria' which, it is feared, could lead to the kind of destruction seen in the forests of North America.[12] Aside from the urgent need to address global warming, a number of measures, all requiring a long-term approach, have been recommended by scientists to tackle these threats and to try, especially with regard to man-made plantations, to develop more resilient populations. These include the planting of mixed stands of trees and thinning out regimented rows of single species to allow for natural regrowth, as well as new management techniques and tighter controls on the international trade in trees. According to Stephen Cavers, there is some 'cause for optimism about the prospect of management measures to lessen the impact of new pests and pathogens', and in northern temperate forests, where trees such as birches are wind pollinated and so can spread their genes widely, populations may adapt.[13]

In addition, birches are able to germinate in soil stripped of its organic layer by the most intense of forest fires, and they may come to take the place of conifers destroyed by fire or disease, whose seeds are unable to germinate, in large areas of the regions they once dominated. Climate change, however – which should perhaps be more appropriately referred to as climate breakdown – will, it seems, only worsen the situation facing a number of individual birch species and distinctive local populations that are now endangered to a lesser or greater extent in various locations around the world. Largely the casualties of human interference resulting in habitat destruction, as well as changing weather patterns, one of these is the Japanese *B. chichibuensis* listed on the IUCN's latest 'Red List of Threatened Species' (2017) as 'critically endangered'.[14] Found only in a few very remote locations in the Chichibu region of Japan in the mountains of central Honshu, this multi-stemmed shrub or small tree, reaching only some 10 m (32 ft) in height, had become so rare that by 1993 just 21 trees were believed to remain in one stand in the wild, a population much too small to sustain itself without help.[15] The species is thought to be of very ancient origin with no close relatives anywhere else in the world.

B. chichibuensis seedlings at Ness Botanic Gardens, offspring of trees grown there from seeds collected from wild birches in Honshu, Japan.

Seed collected in 1986 from these Japanese trees and sent to Britain, however, produced eight young trees, grown at Ness Botanic Gardens in northwest England, from which more trees have been produced and which have been the source of genetic material distributed to arboreta and botanic gardens elsewhere.[16] In a more recent development, in 2014 a joint Anglo-Japanese expedition by Oxford Botanic Garden and the University of Tokyo collected two thousand seeds from one of several additional stands of trees that had been discovered, from which about a hundred seedlings were produced. Further collections of seeds were also made in 2016. The long-term aim of the project is to help restore genetic diversity to the small number of these birches grown in arboreta around the world, thus boosting efforts to save the species in the wild while also raising awareness of the threats to all the world's wild plants.[17]

Clearly, the immediate answer to such threats is to reduce the destruction of the habitat in which birches grow and, with regard to all birch species, manage as best we can the woods and forests they have formed or populated for so long, allowing them to expand naturally where possible and restraining predators such as deer and sheep. Birches, we should not forget, have proved themselves to be great survivors. Because of the breakdown in the traditional management of British woodlands that has occurred over the last century, and which has caused the competitive ability of other trees to decline, Oliver Rackham felt able to conclude:

> The birches have come to stay and are likely to increase further. It is a pity that so little use should be made of a beautiful and potentially valuable tree which grows whether we want it or not and costs nothing.[18]

Timeline

c. 70 million years ago	Pollen resembling that produced by birches and their closest relatives, alders, in existence. Betulaceae family common across the northern hemisphere
c. 50 million years ago	Birches exist as a separate genus: *Betula*. Oldest known fossil birch is *B. leopoldae*
c. 260,000–250,000 BCE	Birch tar produced in the Upper Valdarno Basin, Italy, may be the first synthetic product ever made by humans
c. 120,000 BCE	Birch tar being used in Germany, probably as an adhesive for tool manufacture
c. 10,000 BCE	Birches are the first trees to return to Britain and form forest on their own as ice sheets retreat
c. 7000 BCE	Birch tar being chewed in Germany, Scandinavia and other parts of Europe, possibly for medicinal purposes
3300 BCE	Ötzi the Iceman from the Italian/Austrian border carries birch bark containers and birch polypore (*Fomitopsis betulina*) fungus, and uses birch tar as a glue and sealant for his tools and weapons
First century CE	Gandharan Buddhist texts written on birch bark – earliest known versions of important Buddhist scriptures

92–100 CE	Letters written on thin slivers of birch wood by Romans at Vindolanda, northern Britain
921	Arab traveller Ahmad ibn Fadlan notes fermented birch sap being drunk by the Bulgars of the Volga region in Russia
1260	'Onfim' makes notes and drawings on birch bark at Novgorod, Russia, following a long-established tradition
1500s onwards	Numerous colonial records made of the use of birch bark by Native Americans for canoes, housing, basketry, food, clothing and spiritual purposes
1561	Italian botanist and physician Pietro Andrea Mattioli recommends birch sap and leaves as a treatment for kidney and gall stones
1664	John Evelyn extols the virtues of birch sap wine and lists many traditional uses of birch wood, as well as 'Gallants Sweet-powder'
c. 1750	First birch-bark canoe factory established at Trois-Rivières, Quebec, where huge stockpiles of bark are accumulated
1753	Carl Linnaeus classifies what are now distinguished as the silver birch (*B. pendula*) and downy birch (*B. pubescens*) as *B. alba* (white birch) in *Species Plantarum*
1786	The *Metta Catharina*, a Danish ship carrying a cargo of Russia leather (reindeer hides treated with birch tar oil), sinks off Plymouth Sound
1802	Samuel Taylor Coleridge describes the silver birch as 'The Lady of the Woods' in his poem 'The Picture or the Lover's Resolution'
1880s	Pennsylvania has become an important centre for the production of oil of wintergreen from the sweet birch (*B. lenta*)

1884	Vincent van Gogh creates *Pollard Birches*, a study in pencil, pen and ink and watercolour on paper, as part of a series of studies of the Brabant landscape in the Netherlands
1920s	Centralized collection of birch sap begun in the Soviet Union
1924	Coco Chanel's 'Cuir de Russe' perfume containing birch tar launched
c. 1939–*c.* 1945	Industrial process for production of xylitol from birch wood developed in Finland
1940–50	Mosquito aircraft built of birch and balsa wood, most for combat during the Second World War
1940–56	Letters written on birch bark by Latvian and Lithuanian prisoners in Siberia
1947	The 'Spruce Goose' aeroplane made almost entirely of birch plywood makes its first and only brief flight
1993	Birching laws finally repealed on the Isle of Man
2015	Scientists warn of the serious threats to birches and other trees of the world's boreal forests from new pests and diseases due to climate breakdown
2017	Hanging scroll painting *White Birches on Mount Chang Bai* by Wu Guanzhong sells for £500,000 at auction in Britain

References

Introduction

1 Kenneth Ashburner and Hugh A. McAllister, *The Genus Betula: A Taxonomic Revision of Birches* (London, 2013), p. 306.
2 Tine Schenk and Peter Groom, 'The Aceramic Production of *Betula pubescens* (Downy Birch) Bark Tar Using Simple Raised Structures: A Viable Neanderthal Technique?', *Archaeological and Anthropological Sciences*, X/I (2016).
3 Ray Mears, *Bushcraft*, S02E01 – 'Birchbark Canoe', www.youtube.com, 19 August 2012.
4 Y. A. Dunaev, 'Birches at the Roadside – a Historical Sketch', *Ural Pipe*, 3 (1991), p. 3.
5 Ornäsbjörken, 'Ornäs Birch – Seductive and False', www.ornasbjorken.se, accessed 4 June 2017.
6 New Hampshire, 'New Hampshire Almanac – State Tree', www.nh.gov, accessed 4 June 2017.
7 Ashburner and McAllister, *The Genus Betula*, p. 285.
8 Barbara A. Maher et al., 'Impact of Roadside Tree Lines on Indoor Concentrations of Traffic-derived Particulate Matter', *Environmental Science Technology*, XLVII (2013), pp. 13, 737–44.

1 The Natural History of Birches

1 Kenneth Ashburner and Hugh A. McAllister, *The Genus Betula: A Taxonomic Revision of Birches* (London, 2013), pp. 3–9.
2 Ibid., pp. ix–x.
3 Ibid., pp. 45, 279.
4 George Monbiot, *Feral* (London, 2013), p. 74.
5 Oliver Rackham, *Trees and Woodland in the British Landscape* (London, 1976), pp. 32–3.
6 John Evelyn, *Sylva* (London, 1664), p. 32.
7 Archie Miles, *Silva* (London, 1999), p. 96.
8 Ashburner and McAllister, *The Genus Betula*, pp. 279–80.

9 Oliver Rackham, *Woodlands* (London, 2015), p. 48.
10 Ashburner and McAllister, *The Genus Betula*, p. 306.
11 Derek Ratcliffe, *Lapland: A Natural History* (London, 2005), p. 85.
12 Religious Tract Society, *Visitor or Monthly Instructor* (London, 1842), p. 197.
13 Richard Mabey, *Flora Britannica* (London, 1997), p. 84.
14 Rackham, *Woodlands*, pp. 163, 302.
15 Ashburner and McAllister, *The Genus Betula*, pp. 15, 19.
16 Ibid., p. 5.
17 P. R. Crane and R. A. Stockey, 'Betula Leaves and Reproductive Structures from the Middle Eocene of British Columbia', *Canadian Journal of Botany*, LXV (1987), pp. 2490–500, in Ashburner and McAllister, *The Genus Betula*, p. 48.
18 Ashburner and McAllister, *The Genus Betula*, p. 5.
19 Ibid., p. 18.
20 Ibid., pp. 43, 47–8.
21 R. J. Abbot et al., 'Molecular Analysis of Plant Migration and Refugia in the Arctic', *Science*, CCLXXXIX (2000), pp. 1343–6, in Ashburner and McAllister, *The Genus Betula*, p. 50.
22 Ashburner and McAllister, *The Genus Betula*, p. 50.
23 Ibid., p. 52.
24 H.J.B. Birks, 'British Trees and Insects: a Test of the Time Hypothesis over the last 13,000 years', *American Naturalist*, CXV (1980), pp. 600–605.
25 Oliver Rackham, *Trees and Woodland* (London, 1990), p. 27, and *Woodlands*, p. 71.
26 'Common Silver Birch', www.phadia.com, accessed 3 May 2017.
27 A. G. Gordon, ed., *Seed Manual for Forest Trees* (London, 1992), pp. 74, 94.
28 Ashburner and McAllister, *The Genus Betula*, p. 35.
29 Monbiot, *Feral*, p. 74.
30 Gordon Patterson, *The Value of Birches in Upland Forests for Wildlife Conservation*, Forestry Commission Bulletin, 109 (1993), p. 15; and Ashburner and McAllister, *The Genus Betula*, p. 88.
31. Seppo Lapinjoki et al., 'Development and Structure of Resin Glands on Tissues of *Betula pendula Roth*, During Growth', *New Phytologist*, CXVII (1991), pp. 219–23 and Ashburner and McAllister, *The Genus Betula*, pp. 87, 109.
32 Monbiot, *Feral*, pp. 70, 73–4, 154–60.
33 USDA Forest Service, www.fs.fed.us, 24 May 2010.
34 Ashburner and McAllister, *The Genus Betula*, p. 292.
35 R. B. Harvey, 'Relation of the Color of Bark to the Temperature of the Cambium in Winter', *Ecology*, IV (1923), pp. 391–4, in ibid., p. 103.
36 Monbiot, *Feral*, p. 92.
37 Ibid., pp. 103–4.
38 Ibid., pp. 92–3.
39 W. J. de Groot et al., 'Betula nana L. and Betula glandulosa Michx', *Journal of Ecology*, LXXXV (1997), pp. 241–64, in Ashburner and McAllister, *The Genus Betula*, p. 344.

40 R. E. Graber et. al., 'Maximum Ages of Some Trees and Shrubs on Mount Washington', *Forest Notes*, Society for the Protection of New Hampshire Forests, Summer 1973, pp. 23–4.

41 USDA Natural Resources Conservation Sources, 'Yellow Birch', www.plants.usda.gov, 31 May 2006.

42 Martin Brändle and Roland Brandl, 'Species Richness of Insects and Mites on Trees: Expanding Southwood', *Journal of Animal Ecology*, LXX (2001), pp. 491–504.

43 C.E.J. Kennedy et al., 'The Number of Species of Insects Associated with British Trees: A Re-analysis', *Journal of Animal Ecology*, LIII (1984), pp. 455–78.

44 'Birch, Silver (Betula pendula)', www.woodlandtrust.org.uk, accessed 12 December 2014.

45 C. J. Bibby et al., 'Bird Communities of Highland Birchwoods', *Bird Study*, XXXVI (1989), pp. 123–33.

46 L. O. Safford et. al., 'Paper Birch', www.srs.fs.usda.gov, accessed 26 February 2016.

47 Ashburner and McAllister, *The Genus Betula*, p. 118.

48 Audubon, 'Yellow Bellied Sapsucker', www.audubon.org, accessed 3 March 2016.

2 Tree of Well-being

1 John Evelyn, *Sylva* (London, 1664), p. 33.

2 Ingvar Svanberg et al., 'Uses of Tree Saps in Northern and Eastern Parts of Europe', *Acta Societas Botanicorum Poloniae*, LXXXI (2012), pp. 343–57, p. 343.

3 Ibid., p. 343.

4 Ibid., p. 344.

5 Ibid., p. 343.

6 Harriet V. Kuhnlein and Nancy J. Turner, *Traditional Plant Foods of Canadian Indigenous Peoples, Food and Nutrition in History and Anthropology*, vol. VIII (Amsterdam, 1991), pp. 90–91.

7 Nóra Papp et al., 'The uses of *Betula pendula* Roth Among the Hungarian Csángós and Székelys in Transylvania', *Acta Societas Botanicorum Poloniae*, LXXXIII (2014), pp. 113–22, p. 114.

8 Mara Kuka et al., 'Determination of Bioactive Compounds and Mineral Substances in Latvian Birch and Maple Saps', *Proceedings of the Latvian Academy of Sciences*, LXVII (2013), pp. 437–41.

9 Blackdown Cellar, 'Silver Birch Vodka', www.blackdowncellar.co.uk, accessed 10 April 2017.

10 Lukasz Lucazaj et al., 'Sugar Content in the Sap of Birches, Hornbeams and Maples in Southeastern Poland', *Central European Journal of Biology*, IX (2014), pp. 410–16, p. 413.

11 William Milliken and Sam Bridgewater, *Flora Celtica* (Edinburgh, 2013), p. 58.

12 D. D. Henning, 'Maple Sugaring: History of a Folk Technology', *Keystone Folklore Quarterly*, XI (1966), pp. 239–74.

13 'About Birch Syrup', www.alaskabirchsyrup.com, accessed 8 April 2016.
14 Evelyn, *Sylva*, p. 33.
15 John Worlidge, *Vinetum Britannicum* (London, 1678), p. 175.
16 Svanberg et al., 'Uses of Tree Saps', p. 349.
17 Ibid., p. 349.
18 Ibid., p. 348.
19 Ibid., p. 344.
20 Chris Howkins, *Heathland Harvest: The Uses of Heathland Plants Through the Ages* (Addlestone, 1997), p. 11.
21 Nicholas Culpepper, *Culpepper's Complete Herbal* (Manchester, 1826), p. 18.
22 Evelyn, *Sylva*, p. 33.
23 sc *Magazine*, 'As Pure as Birch', www.sibberi.com, accessed 6 April 2017; Clara Vaisse, 'Why You Should Drink Water from Trees', www.newfoodmagazine.com, 17 February 2017.
24 'News – Bernadette Dowling', www.priestlandsbirch.co.uk, accessed 11 March 2016.
25 Svanberg et al., 'Uses of Tree Saps', p. 347.
26 Masahiro Moriyama et al., 'Effect of Birch (Betula platyphylla Sukatchev var. japonica Hara) Sap on Cultured Human Epidermal Keratinocyte Differentiation', *International Journal of Cosmetic Science*, XXXXII (2008), pp. 94–101.
27 M. P. Germano et al., '*Betula pendula* Leaves: Polyphenolic Characterization and Potential Innovative Use in Skin Whitening Products', *Fitoterapia*, LXXXIII (2012), pp. 877–82.
28 Svanberg et al., 'Uses of Tree Saps', p. 351.
29 Subha Rastogi et al., 'Medicinal Plants of the Genus Betula – Traditional Uses and a Phytochemical-pharmacological Review', *Journal of Ethnopharmacology*, CLIX (2015), pp. 62–83, p. 65.
30 Milliken and Bridgewater, *Flora Celtica*, p. 57.
31 Svanberg et al., 'Uses of Tree Saps', p. 350.
32 Birch Sap Festival, https://vk.com/birchsapfest, accessed 15 May 2016.
33 Olga Zyryanova et al., 'White Birch Trees as Resource Species of Russia: their Distribution, Ecophysical Features, Multiple Utilizations', *Eurasian Journal of Forest Research*, XIII (2010), pp. 25–40; Rastogi et al., 'Medicinal Plants of the Genus Betula', pp. 65–6.
34 A. Baumgartner et al., 'Genotoxicity Assessment of Birch-Bark Tar – A Most Versatile Prehistoric Adhesive', *Advances in Anthropology*, 11 (2012), pp. 49–56, p. 50; and Papp et al., 'The Uses of *Betula pendula*', p. 115.
35 Charlotte Erichsen-Brown, *Medicinal and Other Uses of North American Plants: A Historical Survey with Special Reference to the Eastern Indian Tribes* (New York, 1979), p. 47.
36 Ibid., p. 46.
37 Zyryanova et. al., 'White Birch Trees', p. 27.
38 Rastogi et al., 'Medicinal Plants of the Genus Betula', pp. 65–6.
39 Erichsen-Brown, *Medicinal and Other Uses of North American Plants*, pp. 39, 42.

40 Baumgartner et al., 'Genotoxicity Assessment of Birch-Bark Tar', p. 50.
41 Papp et al., 'The Uses of *Betula pendula*', p. 117.
42 Zyryanova et al., 'White Birch Trees', p. 30.
43 Tine Schenk and Peter Groom, 'The Aceramic Production of *Betula pubescens* (Downy Birch) Bark Tar Using Simple Raised Structures: A Viable Neanderthal Technique?', *Archaeological and Anthropological Sciences*, X/1 (2016).
44 Ibid.
45 David. E. Robinson, 'Exploitation of Plant Resources in the Mesolithic and Neolithic of Southern Scandinavia: From Gathering to Harvesting', in *The Origins and Spread of Domestic Plants in Southwest Asia and Europe*, ed. S. Colledge and J. Conolly (London, 2007), p. 367.
46 Elizabeth Aveling, 'Chew, Chew that Ancient Chewing Gum', *British Archaeology* (1997), XXI, p. 6.
47 Baumgartner et al., 'Genotoxicity Assessment of Birch-Bark Tar', p. 50.
48 Zyryanova et al., 'White Birch Trees', p. 30.
49 Baumgartner et al., 'Genotoxicity Assessment of Birch-Bark Tar', pp. 49–56.
50 Tanya M. Barnes and Kerryn A. Greive, 'Topical Pine Tar: History, Properties and Use as a Treatment for Common Skin Conditions', *Australasian Journal of Dermatology*, LVIII (2016), pp. 80–85, p. 82.
51 Rastogi et al., 'Medicinal Plants of the Genus Betula', p. 77.
52 Barnes and Grieve, 'Topical Pine Tar', p. 83.
53 Alakurtti Sami et al., 'Pharmacological Properties of the Ubiquitous Natural Product Betulin', *European Journal of Pharmaceutical Sciences*, XXIX (2006), pp. 1–13.
54 T. P. Shakhtshneider et al., 'New Composites of Betulin Esters with Arabinogalactan as Highly Potent Anti-cancer Agents', *Natural Product Research*, XXX (2016), pp. 1382–7.
55 Sami et al., 'Pharmacological Properties', pp. 1, 11; Wojciech Rzeski et al., 'Betulin Elicits Anti-cancer Effects in Tumour Primary Cultures and Cell Lines in Vitro', Nordic Pharmacological Society, *Basic and Clinical Pharmacology and Toxicology*, CV (2009), pp. 425–32.
56 Rastogi et al., 'Medicinal Plants of the Genus Betula', pp. 62, 75–6, 78–9.
57 Rzeski et al., 'Betulin Elicits Anti-cancer Effects', p. 425; Sami et al., 'Pharmacological Properties', pp. 1, 10.
58 Jing-Jie Tang et al., 'Inhibition of SREBP by a Small Molecule, Betulin, Improves Hyperlipidemia and Insulin Resistance and Reduces Atherosclerotic Plaques', *Cell Metabolism*, XIII (2011), pp. 44–56.
59 Federica Casetti et al., 'Dermocosmetics for Dry Skin: A New Role for Botanical Extracts', *Skin Pharmacology and Physiology*, XXXIV (2011), pp. 289–93, p. 290.
60 Sanna-Maija Miettinen, ed., 'Final Report Summary – FORESTSPECS (*Wood Bark and Peat Based Bioactive Compounds, Speciality Chemicals, and*

Remediation Materials: from Innovations to Applications)' (Finland, 2014), pp. 1–20.

61 Baikal Herbs Ltd, 'Chaga and Other Natural Extracts from Russian Siberia', www.chagatrade.ru, accessed 16 June 2016.

62 Zyryanova et al., 'White Birch Trees', p. 30.

63 Weifa Zheng et al., 'Chemical Diversity of Biologically Active Metabolites in the Sclerotia of Inonotus obliquus and Submerged Culture Strategies for Up-regulating their Production', *Applied Microbiology and Biotechnology*, LXXXVII (2010), pp. 1237–54, pp. 1237–8.

64 Alexander Solzhenitsyn, *Cancer Ward* (London 1968), pp. 157, 161.

65 Yong Sun et al., 'In Vitro Antitumor Activity and Structure Characterization of Ethanol Extracts from Wild and Cultivated Chaga Medicinal Mushroom, Inonotus obliquus', *International Journal of Medicinal Mushrooms*, XIII (2011), pp. 121–30.

66 Zheng et. al., 'Chemical Diversity', pp. 1237–54.

67 Ibid., p. 1238.

68 Ron Spinosa, 'The Chaga Story', *The Mycophile*, XLVII (2006), pp. 1–23, p. 23.

69 South Tyrol Museum of Archaeology, www.iceman.it, accessed 7 October 2016.

70 Marc Barton, 'The Coldest Case – Lessons from the Iceman', www.pastmedicalhistory.co.uk, 26 February 2016.

71 Luigi Capasso, '5300 Years Ago, the Ice Man used Natural Laxatives and Antibiotics', *Lancet*, CCCLII (1998), p. 1864.

72 Robert Rogers, 'Three Under-utilized Medicinal Polypores', *Journal of the American Herbalists Guild*, XII/2 (2014), pp. 15–21, p. 18.

73 Ibid., p. 19.

74 Ursula Peintner and Reinhold Pöder, 'Ethnomycological Remarks on the Iceman's Fungi', in *The Man in the Ice*, ed. S. Bortenschlager and K. Oeggl (Vienna, 2000), pp. 143–50, p. 146.

75 Ibid., p. 148.

76 DuPont, 'XIVIA™ Sweetener is the Tasty, Healthy Option for Xylitol Gum and Candy', www.dupont.com, accessed 6 April 2016.

77 Danisco XIVIA™ White Paper, 'Sustainable and Substantiated for more Sustainable, Healthier Products', www.danisco.com (2012), pp. 1–12, p. 10.

78 'Xylitol – A Global Market Overview', www.prnewswire.com, 17 January 2017.

79 Xylose upstream supply chain information, private communication from Mikkel Thrane, 13 May 2016.

80 Kauko K. Mäkinen, 'History, Safety and Dental Properties of Xylitol', www.globalsweet.com, accessed 6 April 2016.

81 Kauko K. Mäkinen, 'The Rocky Road of Xylitol to its Clinical Application', *Journal of Dental Research*, LXXIX (2000), pp. 1352–5, p. 1352.

82 Duygu Tuncer et al., 'Effect of Chewing Gums with Xylitol, Sorbitol and Xylitolsorbitol on the Remineralization and Hardness of Initial

Enamel Lesions in Situ', *Dental Research Journal*, XI (2014), pp. 537–43, p. 541.
83 Steffen Mickenautsch et al., 'Sugar-free Chewing Gum and Dental Caries – A Systematic Review', *Journal of Applied Oral Science*, XV (2007), pp. 83–8.

3 Practical Birch: Materials for Life

1 Ray Mears, *Bushcraft*, S02E01 – 'Birchbark Canoe', www.youtube.com, 19 August 2012.
2 William Turner, *A New Herball* (London, 1551).
3 Leslie M. Johnson Gottesfeld, 'The Importance of Bark Products in the Aboriginal Economies of Northwestern British Columbia, Canada', *Economic Botany*, XLVI (1992), pp. 148–57, p. 154; Charlotte Erichsen-Brown, *Medicinal and Other Uses of North American Plants: A Historical Survey with Special Reference to the Eastern Indian Tribes* (New York, 1979), p. 43.
4 John C. Loudon, *Arboretum et Fruticetum Britannicum*, vol. III (London, 1838), p. 1697.
5 South Tyrol Museum of Archaeology, www.iceman.it, accessed 5 October 2016.
6 'Historical Knowledge – The Egtved Girl', http://en.natmus.dk, accessed 26 October 2016.
7 Peter D. Jordan, *Material Culture and Sacred Landscape: The Anthropology of the Siberian Khanty* (Walnut Creek, CA, 2003), p. 205.
8 Erichsen-Brown, *Medicinal and Other Uses of North American Plants*, p. 43.
9 Patricia S. Holloway and Ginny Alexander, 'Ethnobotany of the Fort Yukon Region, Alaska', *Economic Botany*, XLIV (1990), pp. 214–25, p. 217.
10 Maan Rokaya et al., 'Ethnobotanical Study of Medicinal Plants from the Humla District of Western Nepal', *Journal of Ethnopharmacology*, CXXX (2010), pp. 485–504.
11 D. Urem-Kotsu et al., 'Birch-bark Tar at Neolithic Makriyalos', Greece, *Antiquity*, LXXVI (2002), pp. 962–7.
12 Erichsen-Brown, *Medicinal and Other Uses of North American Plants*, p. 42.
13 James White, ed., *Handbook of Indians of Canada*, published as an appendix to the Tenth Report of the Geographic Board of Canada, Ottawa, 1913, pp. 55–6.
14 Gottesfeld, 'The Importance of Bark Products', pp. 148–57, p. 150.
15 U. P. Hedric, ed., *Sturtevant's Notes on Edible Plants*, State of New York Department of Agriculture, Twenty-seventh Annual Report, vol. II (Albany, 1919), p. 95.
16 O. Zackrisson et al., 'The Ancient Use of *Pinus sylvestris* L. (Scots pine) Inner Bark by Sami People in Northern Sweden, Related to Cultural and Ecological Factors', *Vegetation History and Archaeobotany*, IX (2000), pp. 99–109.
17 Julie's Kitchen, 'Bark Bread is Back', www.nordicwellbeing.com, 9 January 2011.

18 *Musketry Regulations, Part I*, His Majesty's Stationery Office (London, 1909), pp. 34–5.

19 All About Moose, 'Birch Bark Moose Calls', www.all-about-moose.com, accessed 2 November 2016.

20 Jenny McCune and Hew D. V. Prendergast, 'Betula Makes Music in Europe: Three Birch Horns From Kew's Economic Botany Collections', *Economic Botany*, LVI (2002), pp. 303–5.

21 Minna Hokka, www.minnahokka.com, personal communication, 10 March 2017.

22 Internet Encyclopedia of Ukraine, www.encyclopediaofukraine.com, accessed 13 March 2017.

23 McCune and Prendergast, 'Betula Makes Music in Europe', p. 303; 'The Wooden Lurs', http://abel.hive.no, accessed 13 March 2017.

24 Lurmakaren i Tällberg, 'Näverlurar', www.lurmakaren.se, accessed 13 March 2017.

25 FMQ, 'Music for Cows and Wolves', www.fmq.fi, 7 October 2016.

26 Juhanna Nyrhinen, masauniverse.tumblr.com, personal communication, 10 November 2017; Minna Hokka, www.minnahokka.com, personal communication, 10 March 2017.

27 Erichsen-Brown, *Medicinal and Other Uses of North American Plants*, p. 44.

28 Edward Harding, *The Costume of the Russian Empire* (London, 1803), plate VIII.

29 Loudon, *Arboretum et Fruticetum Britannicum*, vol. III, p. 1709.

30 Birkebeiner, 'The Birkebeiner History', www.birkebeiner.no, accessed 8 November 2016.

31 John L. Peyton, *The Birch: Bright Tree of Life and Legend* (Blacksburg, VA, 1994), p. 39.

32 North House Folk School, *Celebrating Birch: The Lore, Art, and Craft of an Ancient Tree* (Petersburg, PA, 2007), pp. 5–6.

33 Antonina Koshcheeva, 'Revival of Ancient Art of Birch Bark Carving in Western Siberia', www.siberiantimes.com, 25 September 2015.

34 G. J. Cleverley, 'Leather Goods', www.georgecleverley.com, accessed 10 October 2016; The Honourable Cordwainers Company, Guild Library, 'Production of Russia Leather', www.thehcc.org, accessed 27 September 2016.

35 Mears, *Bushcraft*, S02E01.

36 Timothy J. Kent, 'Canoe Manufacturing Materials', http://timothyjkent. com, and 'The History of the Canoe', www.canoe.ca, accessed 10 November 2016.

37 Mears, *Bushcraft*, S02E01.

38 Kent, 'Canoe Manufacturing Materials', and 'The History of the Canoe'.

39 Holloway and Alexander, 'Ethnobotany of the Fort Yukon Region, Alaska', p. 217; Kent, 'Canoe Manufacturing Materials'.

40 Erichsen-Brown, *Medicinal and Other Uses of North American Plants*, p. 39.

41 The Canadian Encyclopedia, *Beothuk*, www.thecanadianencyclopedia.ca, accessed 11 November 2016.

42 Loudon, *Arboretum et Fruticetum Britannicum*, vol. III, p. 1696.

43 Spoken Sanskrit Dictionary, www.spokensanskrit.de, accessed
    1 December 2016.
44 'Kashmir Source for Birch-bark used in Indus Writing',
    www.deccanherald.com, 24 December 2011.
45 William Crooke, *The Popular Religion and Folklore of Northern India*, 11
    (London, 1896), p. 114.
46 N. S. Chauhan, *Medicinal and Aromatic Plants of Himachal Pradesh* (New Delhi,
    1999), p. 127.
47 Kenneth Ashburner and Hugh A. McAllister, *The Genus Betula: A Taxonomic
    Revision of Birches* (London, 2013), p. 248.
48 Online Novgorod, 'General Information', www.novgorod.ru, accessed
    23 November 2016.
49 David M. Herszenhorn, 'Where Mud Is Archaeological Gold, Russian
    History Grew on Trees', *New York Times* (18 October 2014).
50 Latvian National Register, 'In Siberia Written Letters on Birch Bark',
    www.atmina.unesco.lv, accessed 23 November 2016.
51 Moravian Museum, 'Letters from Siberia Written on Birch Bark',
    www.mzm.cz, accessed 5 May 2017.
52 James White, ed., *Handbook of Indians of Canada*, pp. 55–6; Erichsen-Brown,
    Medicinal and Other Uses of North American Plants, p. 42.
53 Erichsen-Brown, p. 38.
54 Ibid., p. 40.
55 Peyton, *The Birch*, p. 59.
56 Erichsen-Brown, *Medicinal and Other Uses*, p. 41.
57 Ibid., p. 39.
58 Vindolanda Trust, www.vindolanda.com, accessed 28 November 2016.
59 Mike Ibeji, 'Vindolanda', www.bbc.co.uk, 16 November 2012.
60 Vindolanda Trust, *If the Shoe Fits*, www.vindolanda.com, 10 October 2016.
61 Basketry and Beyond, 'Farming: Tamar Valley Chip Baskets',
    www.basketryandbeyond.org.uk, accessed 11 November 2016; 'Tamar
    Valley Chip Baskets', http://basketmakerssouthwest.org.uk; Maurice
    Bichard, *Baskets in Europe* (Abingdon, 2008), pp. 201–2.
62 Stephen Wilkinson, 'The Miraculous Mosquito', www.historynet.com,
    1 August 2015.
63 The Aviation Zone, 'Hughes HK-1 (H4) "Spruce Goose"',
    www.theaviationzone.com, accessed 30 November 2016.
64 Words attributed to Howard Hughes testifying in 1947 to the Senate
    Special Committee to Investigate the National Defense Program.
65 Howard Mansfield, *Skylark: The Life, Lies and Inventions of Harry Atwood*
    (Hanover, NH, and London, 1999), p. 132.
66 Ibid., p. 132.
67 Ibid., pp. 153–4.
68 Giacinta Bradley Koontz, 'Layers of Wood and Insanity – One Tree
    Flying', www.dommagazine.com, 1 November 2016.
69 Tim Wood, Swindon Aircraft Timber Company, personal
    communication, 5 December 2016.

70 Stone Lane Gardens, 'Practical Uses for Birch', stonelanegardens.com, accessed 30 June 2016.
71 David Prakel, BBC Home Service, 'Hi-Fi Answers' (August 1979), pp. 67–9, p. 67.
72 Ibid., p. 68.
73 Duran Ritz, 'What is the Best Wood for Drum Shells', www.thenewdrummer.com, 26 August 2014.
74 Chris Howkins, *Heathland Harvest: The Uses of Heathland Plants Through the Ages* (Addlestone, 1997), p. 9; H. L. Edlin, *Woodland Crafts in Britain* (London, 1949), pp. 40–42.
75 John Evelyn, *Sylva* (London, 1664), p. 32.
76 Ibid., p. 32.
77 John Evelyn, *Sylva*, ed. Alexander Hunter (London, 1825), p. 143.
78 Loudon, *Arboretum et Fruticetum Britannicum*, vol. III, p. 1699.
79 Edlin, *Woodland Crafts in Britain*, p. 42.
80 Karoliina Niemi, 'Deciduous Tree Species for Sustainable Future Forestry', Nordic-Baltic Forest Conference: Wise Use of Improved Forest Reproductive Material, Riga, 15 September 2015, www.nordgen.org, accessed 2 December 2016.
81 Loudon, *Arboretum et Fruticetum Britannicum*, vol. III, p. 1697.
82 Ibid., p. 1699.
83 Ibid., p. 1698.
84 Olga Zyryanova et al., 'White Birch Trees as Resource Species of Russia', *Eurasian Journal of Forest Research*, XIII (2010), p. 26.
85 Hew D. V. Prendergast and Helen Sanderson, *Britain's Wild Harvest* (London, 2004), p. 35.
86 Edlin, *Woodland Crafts in Britain*, p. 43.
87 Jo Draper, *Pots, Brooms and Hurdles from the Heathlands* (Verwood, 2002), pp. 25–8.
88 Edlin, *Woodland Crafts in Britain*, pp. 43–4.
89 Loudon, *Arboretum et Fruticetum Britannicum*, vol. III, p. 1690.
90 West Highland Museum, 'The Birching Table', www.westhighlandmuseum.org.uk, accessed 9 January 2017.
91 C. Farrell, 'Birching in the Isle of Man 1945 to 1976', www.corpun.com, accessed 9 January 2017.

4 Sacred Birch: Folklore and Tradition

1 John Evelyn, *Sylva*, ed. Alexander Hunter (London, 1825), p. 229.
2 Niall Mac Coitir, *Irish Trees: Myths, Legends and Folklore* (Cork, 2003), p. 22.
3 Alexander Carmichael, *Carmina gadelica* (Edinburgh, 1900), vol. I, p. 172.
4 Kevin Danaher, *The Year in Ireland* (Cork, 1972), p. 96.
5 Richard Mabey, *Flora Britannica* (London, 1997), p. 209.
6 Kenneth Jackson, ed., *A Celtic Miscellany: Translations from Celtic Literatures* (London, 1971), p. 82.

7   Mac Coitir, *Irish Trees*, p. 24.
8   Danaher, *The Year in Ireland*, p. 94.
9   James G. Frazer, *The Golden Bough: A Study in Comparative Religion*, vol. 11 (Cambridge, 2012), p. 66.
10 Mac Coitir, *Irish Trees*, p. 24.
11 Frazer, *The Golden Bough*, p. 64.
12 Ibid.
13 Ibid.
14 Linda J. Ivanits, *Russian Folk Belief* (New York, 1989), pp. 77–80.
15 Frazer, *The Golden Bough*, pp. 64–5.
16 Evelyn, *Sylva*, p. 33.
17 Ingvar Svanberg et al., 'Uses of Tree Saps in Northern and Eastern Parts of Europe', *Acta Societas Botanicorum Poloniae*, LXXXI (2012), pp. 343–57, p. 348.
18 Roy Vickery, *Oxford Dictionary of Plant-Lore* (Oxford, 1995), p. 32.
19 Nóra Papp et al, 'The Uses of *Betula pendula* Roth among the Hungarian Csángós and Székelys in Transylvania, Romania', *Acta Societas Botanicorum Poloniae*, LXXXIII (2014), pp. 113–22, p. 118.
20 Rural Association Support Programme, 'Traditional Celebrations in Novosej, Shishtavec Commune, on 5th and 6th of May', www.rasp.org.al, 23 January 2017.
21 Traian Stoianovich, *Balkan Worlds: The First and Last Europe* (London and New York, 2015), pp. 39–41.
22 Ibid., p. 40.
23 W. E. Tate, *The Parish Chest* (Cambridge, 1946), p. 74.
24 Religious Tract Society, *Visitor or Monthly Instructor* (London, 1842), p. 197.
25 Binche Musée International Du Carnival et du Masque, Pedagogical Activities 308.pdf, www.museedumasque.be; Carnaval de Binche, www.carnavaldebinche.be, accessed 24 January 2017.
26 Papp et al., 'The Uses of *Betula pendula*', p. 118.
27 Frazer, *The Golden Bough*, p. 55.
28 George Calder, *Auraicept na n-Éces: The Scholar's Primer* (Dublin, 1995), pp. 273–4.
29 Peter B. Ellis, 'The Fabrication of "Celtic" Astrology', *The Astrological Journal*, XXXIX (1997), http://cura.free.fr, accessed 16 January 2017.
30 Douglas F. Hulmes, 'Sacred Trees of Norway and Sweden: A Friluftslivquest', http://norwegianjournaloffriluftsliv.com, accessed 18 January 2017.
31 Olga Zyryanova et al., 'White Birch Trees as Resource Species of Russia', *Eurasian Journal of Forest Research*, XIII (2010), p. 25.
32 Gary R. Varner, *The Mythic Forest, the Green Man and the Spirit of Nature* (New York, 2006), p. 57.
33 Andrei Znamenski, *Shamanism in Siberia: Russian Records of Indigenous Spirituality* (Dordrecht, 2003), p. 46.
34 Kevin Turner, *Sky Shamans of Mongolia: Meetings with Remarkable Healers* (Berkeley, CA, 2016), p. 152.

35 Alexander Newby, 'Sushi with a Shaman', www.transformsiberia.
wordpress.com, accessed 14 May 2017.
36 Varner, *The Mythic Forest*, p. 57.
37 Arctic Photo, 'Arctic Native Peoples: Yakut', www.arcticphoto.com,
accessed 31 January 2017.
38 John L. Peyton, *The Birch: Bright Tree of Life and Legend* (Blacksburg, VA,
1994), p. 33.
39 Glenn H. Shephard Jr, 'Psychoactive Botanicals in Ritual, Religion and
Shamanism', in *Ethnopharmacology: Encyclopedia of Life Support Systems* (EOLSS),
vol. II, ed. Elaine Elisabetsky and Nina Elkin (Oxford, 2005).
40 BBC Natural Histories, 'Fly Agaric', www.bbc.co.uk, accessed
31 January 2017.
41 Peyton, *The Birch*, p. 32.
42 Simply Baskets, 'Information About Russian Birch Bark Box Crafts',
www.simplybaskets.com, 14 February 2017.
43 Frances Densmore, *Strength of the Earth: The Classic Guide to Ojibwe Uses
of Native Plants* (St Paul, MN, 2005), p. 381.
44 Ibid., pp. 381–4.

5 The Lady of the Woods: Images of Birch

1 Terry Gifford, *Pastoral* (London, 1999), p. 109.
2 Niall Mac Coitir, *Irish Trees: Myths, Legends and Folklore* (Cork, 2003), p. 26.
3 Ibid., p. 24.
4 Nicholas Culpepper, *Culpepper's Complete Herbal* (Manchester, 1826),
p. 18
5 Kenneth Jackson, ed., *A Celtic Miscellany* (1971), pp. 83–4.
6 John Beer, *Coleridge's Play of Mind* (Oxford, 2010), p. 94.
7 Stephanie Forward, 'The Romantics', in *Discovering Literature: Romantics and
Victorians*, www.bl.uk, 15 May 2014.
8 Constance Naden, 'Poesy Club', *Mason College Magazine*, 4.5 (October 1886),
p. 106.
9 Geoffrey Durrant, *Wordsworth and the Great System: A Study of Wordsworth's
Poetic Universe* (Cambridge, 1970), pp. 77–8.
10 Oliver Rackham, *Ancient Woodland: Its History, Vegetation and Uses in England*
(London, 1980), p. 311.
11 Jenny McCune and Hew D. V. Prendergast, 'Betula Makes Music in
Europe: Three Birch Horns From Kew's Economic Botany Collections',
Economic Botany, LVI (2002), pp. 303–5, p. 304.
12 Internet Sacred Text Archive, Legends/Sagas, Northern European,
Finland, *The Kalevala*, 'Rune XLIV. Birth of the Second Harp',
www.sacred-texts.com, accessed 28 May 2017.
13 Olga Zyryanova et al., 'White Birch Trees as Resource Species of Russia',
Eurasian Journal of Forest Research, XIII (2010), p. 25.
14 M. Pittock, 'Thresholds of Memory: Birch and Hawthorn', *European
Romantic Review*, XXVII (2016), pp. 449–58.

15 SparkNotes, 'Frost's Early Poems: "Birches"', www.sparknotes.com, accessed 1 June 2017.

16 Accordeonworld, Russian Songs and Their History, 'Beriozka', http://accordeonworld.weebly.com, accessed 2 June 2017.

17 R. H. Pearce, *Savagism and Civilization: A Study of the Indian and the American Mind* (Berkeley and Los Angeles, CA, 1988), p. 192.

18 Nan Shepherd, *The Living Mountain* (Edinburgh, 2011), pp. xiii.

19 Tate Britain, 'Millais, *The Knight Errant*', www.tate.org.uk, accessed 12 June 2017.

20 Manchester Galleries, Collections, 'Millais, *Winter Fuel*', www.manchesterartgallery.org, accessed 12 June 2017.

21 Van Gogh Museum, *Pollard Birches*, www.vangoghmuseum.nl; *Letters to brother Theo*, www.vangoghletters.org, accessed 14 June 2017.

22 Emillions Art, Master Artists, 'Gustav Klimt', www.emillionsart.com, accessed 13 June 2016.

23 Gustav Klimt: Paintings, Quotes and Biography, *Birch Forest I*, 1902 by Gustav Klimt, www.gustav-klimt.com, accessed 14 June 2017.

24 McMichael, *Painting Canada: Tom Thomson and the Group of Seven*, www.mcmichael.com, accessed 14 June 2017.

25 Tom's Legacy, Charles Hill, www.youtube.com, accessed 13 June 2017.

26 'Chinese Paintings Expected to Set a UK Record', *Blackmore Vale Magazine* (5 May 2017), p. 41.

27 Duke's Auctioneers, 'Chinese Masterworks Surface at Dorset Auction', www.dukes-auctions.com, 27 April 2017.

6 The Future of Birch

1 S. Gauthier et al., 'Boreal Forests Challenged by Global Change', International Institute for Applied Systems Analysis, www.iiasa.ac.at, 21 August 2015.

2 'Greenpeace calls for urgent global action to save the Great Northern Forest', www.greenpeace.org, 7 December 2016; Gauthier et al., 'Boreal Forests Challenged'.

3 S. Gauthier et al., 'Boreal Forest Health and Global Change', *Science*, CCCXLIX (2015), pp. 819–22; Tim Appenzeller, 'The New North: Stoked by Climate Change, Fire and Insects are Remaking the Planet's Vast Boreal Forest', *Science*, CCCXLIX (2015), pp. 806–9.

4 Gauthier et al., 'Boreal Forest Health', p. 820.

5 Gauthier et al., 'Boreal Forest Challenged'.

6 Tim Appenzeller, 'The New North'.

7 S. A. Katovich et al., USDA *Forest Service, Forest Insect & Disease Leaflet 111, Bronze Birch Borer*, www.fs.usda.gov, 2000.

8 Katovich et al., *Bronze Birch Borer*; Kenneth Ashburner and Hugh A. McAllister, *The Genus Betula: A Taxonomic Revision of Birches* (London, 2013), p. 87.

9 Bronze Birch Borer (*Agrilus anxius*) Forestry Commission, www.forestry.gov.uk/bronzebirchborer, 13 January 2018.

10 Ian Johnston, 'Trees Under Threat: The Oak, Beech and Birch Could Be Lost If Britain Does Not Act Quickly', *The Independent* (11 January 2015).

11 S. Cavers, 'Evolution, Ecology and Tree Health: Finding Ways to Prepare Britain's Forests for Future Threats', *Forestry*, LXXXVIII (1 January 2015), pp. 1–2.

12 Johnston, 'Trees Under Threat'.

13 Cavers, 'Evolution, Ecology and Tree Health', pp. 1–2.

14 IUCN Red List 2017, www.iucnredlist.org, accessed 20 March 2017.

15 Kenneth Ashburner and Hugh A. McAllister, *The Genus Betula: A Taxonomic Revision of Birches* (London, 2013), p. 137; IUCN Red List 2017, accessed 20 March 2017.

16 Ashburner and McAllister, *The Genus Betula*, pp. 139–40.

17 Rachel Nuwer, 'Saving a Rare Tree Worlds Away', *New York Times*, 26 October 2015.

18 Oliver Rackham, *Ancient Woodland: Its History, Vegetation and Uses in England* (London, 1980), p. 318.

Further Reading

Ashburner, Kenneth, and Hugh A. McAllister, *The Genus Betula: A Taxonomic Revision of Birches* (London, 2013)

Baumgartner, A., et al., 'Genotoxicity Assessment of Birch-Bark Tar – A Most Versatile Prehistoric Adhesive', *Advances in Anthropology*, 11 (2012), pp. 49–56

Culpepper, Nicholas, *Culpepper's Complete Herbal* (Manchester, 1826)

Danaher, Kevin, *The Year in Ireland* (Cork, 1972)

Edlin, H. L., *Woodland Crafts in Britain* (London, 1949)

Erichsen-Brown, Charlotte, *Medicinal and Other Uses of North American Plants: A Historical Survey with Special Reference to the Eastern Indian Tribes* (New York, 1979)

Evelyn, John, *Sylva* (London, 1664)

Frazer, James, G., *The Golden Bough: A Study in Comparative Religion* (Cambridge, 2012)

Hageneder, Fred, *The Heritage of Trees: History, Culture and Symbolism* (Edinburgh, 2001)

—, *The Living Wisdom of Trees* (London, 2005)

Howkins, Chris, *Heathland Harvest: The Uses of Heathland Plants Through the Ages* (Addlestone, 1997)

Loudon, John C., *Arboretum et Fruticetum Britannicum* (London, 1838)

Mabey, Richard, *Flora Britannica* (London, 1997)

Mac Coitir, Niall, *Irish Trees: Myths, Legends and Folklore* (Cork, 2003)

Mansfield, Howard, *Skylark: The Life, Lies and Inventions of Harry Atwood* (Hanover, CT, and London, 1999)

Miles, Archie, *Silva* (London, 1999)

Milliken, William, and Sam Bridgewater, *Flora Celtica* (Edinburgh, 2013)

Monbiot, George, *Feral* (London, 2013)

North House Folk School, *Celebrating Birch: the Lore, Art and Craft of an Ancient Tree* (Petersburg, 2007)

Papp, Nóra, et al., 'The Uses of Betula pendula Roth among Hungarian Csángós and Székelys in Transylvania, Romania', *Acta Societatis Botanicorum Poloniae*, LXXXIII (2014), pp. 113–22

Peyton, John L., *The Birch: Bright Tree of Life and Legend* (Blacksburg, VA, 1994)

Rackham, Oliver, *Ancient Woodland: Its History, Vegetation and Uses in England* (London, 1980)

—, *Trees and Woodland in the British Landscape* (London, 1976 and 1990)

—, *Woodlands* (London, 2015)

Rastogi, Subha et al., 'Medicinal Plants of the Genus Betula – Traditional Uses and a Phytochemical-pharmacological Review', *Journal of Ethnopharmacology*, CLIX (2015), pp. 62–83

Schenk, Tine, and Peter Groom, 'The Aceramic Production of *Betula pubescens* (Downy Birch) Bark Tar Using Simple Raised Structures: A Viable Neanderthal Technique ?', *Archaeological and Anthropological Sciences*, X/1 (2016), pp. 19–29.

Solzhenitsyn, Alexander, *Cancer Ward* (London, 1968)

Svanberg, Ingvar, et al., 'Uses of Tree Saps in Northern and Eastern Parts of Europe', *Acta Societas Botanicorum Poloniae*, LXXXI (2012), pp. 343–57

Turner, Kevin, *Sky Shamans of Mongolia: Meetings with Remarkable Healers* (Berkeley, CA, 2016)

Varner, Gary, *The Mythic Forest, The Green Man and the Spirit of Nature* (New York, 2006)

Vickery, Roy, *Oxford Dictionary of Plant-lore* (Oxford, 1995)

Zyryanova, Olga, et al., 'White Birch Trees as Resource Species of Russia', *Eurasian Journal of Forest Research*, XIII (2010), pp. 25–40

Associations and Websites

ARNOLD ARBORETUM, USA
www.arboretum.harvard.edu

BOTANISKA, GOTHENBURG BOTANICAL GARDEN, SWEDEN
www.botaniska.se

HERGEST CROFT GARDENS
A National Collection holder of birch
www.hergestcroft.co.uk

KEW ECONOMIC BOTANY COLLECTION, ONLINE DATABASE
Large collection of birch artefacts and access to online databases
www.kew.org/science/collections/economic-botany-collection

NESS BOTANIC GARDENS
One of the largest collections of birches in cultivation, including a number
of rare *Betula chichibuensis* from Japan
www.nessgardens.org.uk

PLANTS OF THE WORLD ONLINE
A multi-dimensional catalogue of plant life providing authoritative
information on the world's plant species
www.plantsoftheworldonline.org

ROYAL BOTANIC GARDENS, EDINBURGH
The Birch Lawn
www.rbge.org.uk

STONE LANE GARDENS
A National Collection holder of birch and alder
www.stonelanegardens.com

VON GIMBORN ARBORETUM, NETHERLANDS
www.gimbornarboretum.nl

WAKEHURST PLACE
A National Collection holder of birch
www.kew.org/wakehurst

Acknowledgements

I am very grateful to the many people who helped me to research and write this book. I must start with Hugh McAllister for his advice about the early history and identification of birches and for permission to draw on and quote from the outstanding book of which he is co-author, *The Genus Betula: A Taxonomic Revision of Birches*. This book, which untangles and clarifies the birch's highly complex taxonomy and provides so much other essential information, has been an enormous help throughout, particularly for the writing of my chapter on the natural history of birches. I would have been lost without it. Thank you also to Catherine McAllister for her help, especially with regard to illustrations kindly supplied by Josephine Hague.

My thanks, too, to Arctic expert Bryan Alexander of Arcticphoto for patiently answering my queries about Siberian peoples and their culture: Tim Baxter, University of Liverpool Botanic Gardens, for advice about birch collections; Ian Bower, Assistant Keeper, Great North Museum Library, Tyne & Wear for help accessing William Turner's *A New Herball*; Lynda Brooks, Librarian at the Linnean Society of London, for help concerning the historic consumption of birch bark in Sweden; Dulce Ben-East of Alaska Wild Harvest, for advice about Alaskan birch syrup and for sending delicious samples; Minna Hokka, Rauno Nieminen, Joonas Keskinen, Juhana Nyrhinen and Lari Aaltonen for information about Scandinavian birch bark musical instruments; Günther Kaufmann, Scientific Curator, South Tyrol Museum of Archaeology with regard to Ötzi's use of birch tar; Julie Lindahl for advice about birch bark bread; Karl Morgan of Swansea Museum for help with information about Welsh copper refining; Professor Mark Nesbitt, Economic Botany Research Leader and Economic Botany Collection Curator, Royal Botanic Gardens, Kew, for his advice and help locating useful publications and illustrations and for access to the birch artefacts held within the Economic Botany Collection; Alexander Newby for information about and photos of Buryat shamanic ritual; Jack Pritchard for his notes from the 'Beech and Birch in Natural History, History and Literature' event in Oxford 2015; Mikkel Thrane, Corrina Shaw, Maureen Hall and Kati Kousa, all of DuPont Nutrition and Health, for information about xylitol; Luke Winter, formerly Manager of the Centre for Ancient Technology, Cranborne, for advice about the historic use of birch tar.

Thanks also to Craig Brough, Information Services Librarian, Library, Art and Archives, Royal Botanic Gardens, Kew; Emma Darbyshire, Image Library Assistant, Fitzwilliam Museum, Cambridge; Pipp Dodd, Senior Collections Development and Review Curator (Stevenage), National Army Museum; Keith Dover, County Moth Recorder, County Durham; Kim Edwards, Zhong Wei Horticultural Products Co; William Fletcher, Fletcher Salads, Spalding; Gina Fullerlove, Head of Publishing, Royal Botanic Gardens, Kew; Carl Gawboy; Ester Gaya, Senior Research Leader, Mycology, Royal Botanic Gardens, Kew; Stuart Griffin, Swansea University; Alina Grigorjan, Pushkin House, London; Sara Hannant; Carol Horsington, Basketmakers South West; Ben Jones; Arboretum Curator, University of Oxford Botanic Garden and Arboretum; Tony Kirkham, Head of Arboretum, Gardens and Horticultural Services, Royal Botanic Gardens, Kew; Paul Kirtley, Frontier Bushcraft; Kristine Kusnere, SaunaGoods.com; Adam Law, and Nick Eisa, George Cleverley & Co. Ltd, London; Konnie Le May, Editor, *Lake Superior* magazine; Professor Barbara Maher, Centre for Environmental Magnetism and Palaeomagnetism, Lancaster University; Gemma Meek and John Holmes, Duke's Fine Art Auctioneers, Dorchester; Neil McGregor, Assistant Manager, Doncaster Heritage Services; Dr J. Nasal, Xylitol. org; Pat O'Reilly MBE, First Nature; Dr Subha Rastogi, Senior Scientist, Pharmacognosy and Ethnopharmacology Division, National Botanical Research Institute, Lucknow, India; Professor Ihor Soloviy, Ukrainian National Forestry University; Victor Smirnov, Baikal Herbs Ltd; Paul Smit, photographer and journalist; Konstantin Shlykov, Head of Press Office, Embassy of Russia, London; Nicola Tinsley, Image Library and Research Libraries Co-ordinator, Waddesdon Manor; Clara Vaisse, Sibberi; Kimberley Walker, Economic Botany Collections, Royal Botanic Gardens, Kew; Solomon Wasser, Editor-in-Chief, *International Journal of Medicinal Mushrooms*; Colin Wells; Lydia White, Sales and Marketing Manager, Royal Botanic Gardens, Kew; Keith Whitehead, Woodlore Ltd; Richard Wragg, Archivist, The National Gallery, London.

Friends Gilly Beauclerk, Catherine Broadway, Fanny Charles, Imogen Evans, Suzie Lawrence, Mary Prendergast and Terry Townsend also made valuable contributions, for which I'm very grateful. Sandy Roberts and colleagues at Sturminster Newton Library were always ready to help.

Lastly, thank you to Michael Leaman and his team at Reaktion Books, Edward Parker for suggesting I write this book, my children Eppie and Aaron for their constant encouragement, and John Short for always being there – interpreting and checking statistical information, untangling chemical conundrums, accessing inaccessible documents – and for his tireless practical support.

Photo Acknowledgements

❧

The author and the publishers wish to express their thanks to the below sources of illustrative material and/or permission to reproduce it.

Alamy: pp. 8 (Tim Gainey), 15 (blikwinkel), 18–19 (All Canada Photos), 22 (imageBROKER), 42 (Mykahilo Shcherbyna), 85 (SPUTNIK), 121 (Angela Hampton), 140 (Peter Cavanagh); ArcticPhoto: pp. 77, 146 (B&C Alexander); BAE Systems: p. 110; Baikal Herbs Ltd: p. 61 (Victor Smirnov); Beaver Bark Canoes: p. 95 (Ferdy Goode); British Library: p. 102; © The Trustees of the British Museum, London: p. 99; Andrew Brown and Royal Botanic Gardens, Kew: p. 26 (from Kenneth Ashburner and Hugh A. McAllister, *The Genus Betula: A Taxonomic Revision of Birches*); Pat Bruderer: p. 79; Marian Byrne: p. 100; Calstock Parish Archive: p. 109; Clarke Historical Library, Central Michigan University: p. 78; George Cleverley & Co. Ltd, Bond Street, London: pp. 92, 93; Doncaster Museum Service, Doncaster Metropolitan Borough Council: p. 160; Keith Dover: p. 39; Dreamstime: pp. 14 (Yi Li), 38 (Jozef Jankola), 119 (Sandyprints), 142 (Kaprik); Dukes Fine Art Auctioneers, Dorchester: p. 178; ©The Fitzwilliam Museum, Cambridge: p. 169; Floracopeia.com: p. 55; Foss Distillery: p. 47; Fossilera. com: p. 28; GardenPhotos.com: p. 34 (Graham Rice); Carl Gawboy: p. 151; Arthur Haines: p. 52; Josephine Hague and Royal Botanical Gardens, Kew: p. 29 (from Kenneth Ashburner and Hugh A. McAllister, *The Genus Betula: A Taxonomic Revision of Birches*); Sara Hannant: p. 128; Jörg Hempel: p. 33; Alison Hullyer: p. 177; Hungerford Virtual Museum: p. 139; Hvilya.com: p. 49; iStockphoto: pp. 23 (zigmej), 122 (duncan1890), 130 (HorstBingemer); Kristiina Johanssen: pp. 27, 40; Landesamt für Denkmalpflege und Archäologie Sachsen-Anhalt: p. 58 (Juraj Lipták); Barbara Maher: p. 12; Mountainhikes.com: p. 168 (Kevin Blissett); Courtesy of the Museum of the River Daugava, Latvia: p. 106; National Museum of Art, Architecture and Design, Norway: p. 145 (Jacques Lathion); © National Trust, Waddesdon Manor, Bequest of Dorothy de Rothschild, 1988; ac. No 2953: p. 124; Faculty of Natural Sciences (NTNU): p. 30 (Per Harald Olsen); Nature Picture Library: p. 16 (Bryan and Cherry Alexander); N. S. Nadezhdina Choreographic Ensemble 'Berezka': p. 164; Ness Botanic Gardens: p. 184 (Tim Baxter); New England Wild Flower Society: p. 52 (Arthur Haines); Alexander Newby (tearoadtiger@gmail.com): p. 149; Richard Nicholson, antiquemaps.com: p. 87;

Index

Page numbers in *italics* refer to illustrations.